Advance praise for
The Natural Advantage

"Alan Heeks has done a marvellous job in first mapping out the basic principles of organic farming, and then demonstrating how each of those principles bears directly on the business of running a successful organization. *The Natural Advantage* is both practical in its day-to-day application to management practices, and rich in its philosophical implications."

Jonathon Porritt, Forum for the Future

"*The Natural Advantage* is a brilliant synthesis of biomimicry and psychology to create a living tool that can transform people, the planet and organizations. It is thoroughly practical while providing a powerful array of new possibilities for our relationship with each other and the environment."

Paul G. Hawken, author of Natural Capitalism, The Ecology of Commerce, Growing a Business.

*This book is dedicated to Magdalen Farm, Dorset,
and to the vision of meeting human needs by
natural principles*

The Natural Advantage

Renewing Yourself

Alan Heeks

NICHOLAS BREALEY
PUBLISHING

LONDON

First published by
Nicholas Brealey Publishing in 2000

36 John Street
London
WC1N 2AT, UK
Tel: +44 (0)20 7430 0224
Fax: +44 (0)20 7404 8311

1163 E. Ogden Avenue, Suite 705-229
Naperville
IL 60563-8535, USA
Tel: (888) BREALEY
Fax: (630) 898 3595

http://www.nbrealey-books.com
http://www.thenaturaladvantage.com

ISBN 1-85788-261-X

British Library Cataloguing in Publication Data
A catalogue record for this book is available from the British Library.

*Paper derived from sustainable sources in accordance with the
Nordic Swan standard.*

Printed in Finland by WS Bookwell.

Contents

Acknowledgments

The experience of writing this book has generally been enjoyable and renewing. Most of the book was written in six months from May to October: producing such a demanding crop within a limited time taught me a lot more about human sustainability at work. It also demonstrated the principle that with high support, a high challenge can lead to high output. I am appreciative of the ways I have supported myself, and of the tremendous help I have received from many other people.

The backing from my colleagues at Working Vision has been superb, especially my secretary Lyn Barker, Sallie Mason, and my main business partner, Barry Seward-Thompson. My fortnightly co-coaching sessions with Barry have been a good combination of friendship and professional support, and his experience of applying this model with clients has been an important input to the book. Many thanks also to Roger Kiddle for his research, Garrie Tiedeman for the drawings, and to Glynis Judge.

I have valued both general and specific support from family and friends: especially my brother Richard, my daughters Ella and Fran, my parents, and friends including Henry Fryer, Emma Dunford Wood, Nayyer Hussain, and Rachel Cullen. I have also drawn on a high level of professional support to sustain my ground condition while writing the book. This includes coaching from Anna Rushton, counseling and healing from Jan

Angelo, aromatherapy from Vicki Poole, and herbal remedies from Dedj Leibrandt.

During my career I have had a succession of excellent mentors, who have raised my self-belief and encouraged me to go for my vision. They begin with Roger Lonsdale, my tutor at Balliol College, Oxford when I was an undergraduate, continuing with Graeme Burge at Procter and Gamble. Peter Jansen was an outstanding mentor as well as boss for seven key years of my career, while I was a managing director at Redland and Caradon. He died in 1997, and I hope that my descriptions in this book pay a deserved tribute to his gifts. I am also deeply grateful for the help I have received from my current mentor, Neil Douglas-Klotz, both directly and through his books, *Prayers of the Cosmos* and *Desert Wisdom*.

This book owes much to my workshop and consultancy clients, and also to many friends and contacts in organic farming. I am especially grateful to Peter Foster and Christina Ballinger at Magdalen Farm for their contributions, and for the breadth of intelligence and good humor they bring to their work. Many thanks also to Francis Blake, Mark Measures, Will Best, John Healey, Ginny Mayall, and the previous farmers at Magdalen: Richard van Bentum and Lya Koornneef, and John and Anna Woodward.

I would also like to acknowledge the help I have had from my contacts in the US, including Deben Tobias, Scott Silverman, and Tertius Halsey, who seeded the idea of my writing a book back in 1995. Finally, I would like to express my deep thanks to the many people who have helped with the creation of Magdalen Farm Centre and the Wessex Foundation since 1990, especially my ex-wife Ruth, Sir George Trevelyan, and fellow trustees Giles Chitty, Janice Dolley, and John Harrison.

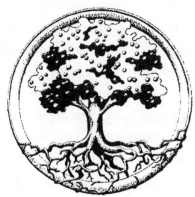

Foreword

Organic farming is now seen as the single most important antidote to the discredited model of postwar intensive farming. Yet for a lot of people, using organic farming as a model for good business management is going to sound pretty strange. It's only in the last couple of years that organic farming has come to be seen as both mainstream and sound business. Before that, it was usually dismissed by farmers, retailers and most politicians as an irrelevant niche market catering for health freaks and tree huggers.

Perhaps the connection between organic farming and good business practice is not self-evident. So take a step back. Organic farming is all about building soil fertility to be able to go on generating nutritious, high-quality produce year after year after year. And good management practices are all about building a culture of creativity and personal fulfillment so that employees are inspired to go on generating high-quality work year after year after year.

Alan Heeks has done a marvelous job in first mapping out the basic principles of organic farming, and then demonstrating how each of those principles bears directly on the business of running a successful organization. By the end, it will all seem perfectly obvious, and if you're anything like me, you'll be asking yourself why you hadn't made those connections before!

In my work at Forum for the Future, one of our main aims is to help businesses to create sustainable solutions to this crisis. Alan has played a valuable role in contributing to some of these programs, combining his wealth of management experience with a fresh and perceptive approach to sustainability.

For me, this book opens up all sorts of new ideas about how to work through the full challenge of sustainable development. We have long argued that sustainable development (which we define as "a dynamic process which enables all people to realize their potential and to improve their quality of life in ways which simultaneously protect and enhance the Earth's life support systems") is as much about people (or human capital) as it is about the planet (or natural capital). Even if we sorted out the environmental crisis, no society (or organization) could be described as truly sustainable if it continued to exploit its citizens (or employees) through political oppression or ruthless profiteering.

Although it is rarely presented in this way, that twin-track approach to sustainable development will eventually permit us to bring our entire way of life into line with the natural rhythm and cycles of nature. Our trajectory as a species cuts directly across those natural systems, wasting, polluting, poisoning, systematically liquidating the "natural capital" on which we depend as utterly as every other species. Realigning that trajectory, by completely reconceptualizing what progress and development really mean, is the greatest challenge we now face.

This is the insight that lies at the heart of *The Natural Advantage*, providing us with a text that is both practical in its day-to-day application to management practices, and rich in its philosophical implications.

Jonathon Porritt
May 2000

1
Forward to Nature

Is your current way of working sustainable? Are you depleting yourself in the drive to produce? Does your work embody human sustainability: increasing output in a way that renews your resources, instead of using them up? If such questions concern you, then this book offers practical answers.

The economic pressure for increased results is unlikely to reduce. Compare the demands your work puts on your capacity now against 10 years ago. Imagine this rate of change doubling in the next 10 years. It's already obvious that the natural environment won't support continued economic growth without radical change in our use of it, and the same is true for human resources.

The environmental impact of our ways of working is clear. Natural physical resources are being depleted and polluted. It's just the same for natural human resources: every company says its people are its greatest resource, but human resources are exhausted and polluted in the production process, just like the natural environment.

My Harvard MBA and senior management career raised more questions than answers about human sustainability, but I have found answers by exploring cultivated natural systems as a model. Since 1990, I have been involved in creating and managing a 130-acre organic farm and this has shown me how natural resources can be used productively and renewably. From this experience, I have evolved *The Natural Advantage*: a set of principles and methods for human sustainability at work.

To meet future growth without burning out, we have to transform energy productivity. The value added per unit of human energy input needs to rise dramatically or we will exhaust ourselves. Organic farming shows how this is possible: free natural energy, waste, and a few non-renewable inputs can be combined in a highly productive system. *The Natural Advantage* shows you how to draw the parallel and raise human energy productivity at work.

The Natural Advantage model is a way of producing more value with less effort. This requires a shift from a linear, mechanistic mindset to a cyclical, organic one: working with natural principles, not overriding them. The linear approach simply applies input A to create output B—end of story. It ignores the depletion and pollution that are by-products of the process. Organic systems choose and use resources so that there is no waste: every output becomes a future input, through the use of natural cycles.

This book offers a new approach to work, a way to increase results while renewing your resources and fulfilling yourself in the process. It sees people and organizations as living organisms, not mechanical systems. By applying *The Natural Advantage* to your work, you will be able to raise your resilience to increasing levels of change and uncertainty. And you will achieve real quality in your outputs—lasting satisfaction for yourself and your customers.

Working with Nature

Rather than going "back to nature," what we need is to go *forward* to nature. This is not a retreatist, downshifting approach, since few of us would want to return to Eden without our house and car. The Natural Advantage comes from working with nature, actively cultivating and shaping it to achieve our productive intent.

We have barely begun to explore how ecology can be used as a model to understand people at work, although a few writers such as Peter Senge and Arie De Geus have started this process. However, the risk when we turn to ecology is to think of wild natural habitats, such as the rainforests. Cultivated natural systems, such as farms, are a much more relevant model, because a farmer is managing natural resources to create economic value sustainably, and this has direct parallels for individuals at work and for organizations.

Outside-in or inside-out?

Mechanistic thinking often leads to outside-in solutions: start with the apparent problem and the desired outcome, then find a technique to fix it. The result is rarely sustainable, since short-term success falls prey to cumulative problems. An organic, systemic approach works from the inside to the outside—from principles to practice, from underlying causes to sustained results. To the organic farmer, both roots and fruits are important, but the roots are the priority. It is by nourishing the roots, maintaining the ground conditions for growth, that we renew the orchard and can expect the fruit to keep coming year after year.

"Working with nature" may sound gentle and easy, but often it isn't. Some forces in a natural system such as the weather can be cruelly destructive or highly unpredictable. There is savage competition as well as exquisite collaboration. The art lies in *managing* your natural resources, using the positive forces of nature to build resilience and achieve a fruitful outcome most of the time.

When I became involved in creating an organic farm in 1990, I was both horrified and fascinated. I had managed some fairly tough businesses, but this was much worse. It felt like driving a car without a steering wheel. In organic farming, it is so clear that you have no control, you can't force things. Instead you have human persistence, ingenuity, and your sense of how to shape natural systems. You learn to read and use the unpredictable forces around you—the weather, pests, weeds, customers, competitors. Organic farming points to the future way of working for all of us: leading and managing with influence, not control, and in situations that are increasingly complex and uncertain.

Intensive or factory farming, where the problems are already apparent, offers alarming insights into the parallel problems of conventional ways of working. Consider the comparison in Table 1 opposite.

Organic farming has benefited from the catastrophic crises in conventional farming. Sales of organic food are reportedly growing at between 50 and 100 percent, with price premiums of 20 to 80 percent over conventional produce. The limitation on sales is how fast supply can be increased. This is a happy story, because by definition organic farmers make their profits sustainably.

The seven principles of organic growth, summarized in the following pages, show how to address the problems of conventional working outlined above. While the application of these principles is different for people at work than for farmers, the organic farm provides a powerful, tangible analogy from which to learn.

The consumer revolt against genetically modified (GM) foods is clear evidence that many people now recognize the

Table 1 The problems of conventional ways of working

Problem	Factory farm	Conventional working
Natural fertility and resources are depleted	Land and livestock	People
Output depends on external pressures	Artificial fertilizers	Deadlines, controls, performance pressures
This creates problems that have to be suppressed	Pests, weeds, diseases treated with pesticides and herbicides	Poor performance met by increased focus on results Stress seen as weakness
Underlying resources are further depleted and polluted	Additive residues pollute ground and groundwater Fertility is reduced	Stress accumulates Vitality, motivation, and resilience are reduced
Output quality is reduced	Product meets nominal standards, but taste and nutrition are poor	Output meets nominal standards, but real quality and satisfaction are poor
Risk of severe problems is increased	Salmonella, BSE, pollution crises	Stress-related illnesses, failure to adapt to change

dangers of the linear, mechanistic model in farming. With time, many of them may see the parallel with the workplace. I hear more and more people and organizations talking about sustainability: the continued tension between economic growth and environmental crisis will force us a long way toward environmental sustainability within the next two decades, if we are to survive. Revolutionary changes in energy and resource use are already apparent. As we start to live sustainably with our environment, this will lead more and more of us to question the human sustainability of work.

The principles of sustainability are the same in every field: individuals, organizations, and the environment. It is ironic that the environmental agenda, and public concern about it, is what is driving most businesses to consider sustainability. Over the next few years, the issues of human and business/economic sustainability will become just as pressing. Organic farming shows us how to address these issues too.

Origins

My interest in how people can fulfill themselves in an economic system began on the first day of my career, when I joined the marketing group of Procter and Gamble in 1969. I was a free spirit fresh from reading English at Oxford, believing that work would be creative, worthwhile, and fun. So P & G was a shock: it was a cold, mechanistic company, which researched and analyzed everything, even the size of nozzle on a Fairy Liquid bottle. It was like a big factory farm, running like clockwork, wound up but efficient. I played the game successfully, but left in 1973, determined to find a better way to work.

I went on to do an MBA at Harvard Business School. This was the business equivalent of joining the Marines. It gave me strength and speed in handling complex new situations, as well as an impressive label. I was also able to explore how work could be made fit for human consumption. This area was called "job enrichment" in the mid-1970s, and some of the pioneering research was by Harvard professors like Lawrence and Lorsch.

After Harvard, I decided that working for a high-powered management consultancy such as McKinsey would not sustain me, despite the fat salary. I took a job at one of the lowest pay levels in the Harvard Class of '76, determined to try my ideas out as a line manager in a company that actually made things. I went to Merseyside, a depressed area of northwest England, as marketing manager of Hygena, a large, loss-making producer of kitchen furniture. From here I moved through two jobs to become managing director of a subsidiary of Redland, one of the UK's largest building materials groups.

The high point of my management career was with Caradon plc between 1985 and 1989. I was a co-founder of this major building materials group, and managing director of the largest subsidiary, Twyfords Bathrooms, which employed 1,500 people. I am proud of the transformation I achieved in Twyfords' morale, profits, and market position. Starting a business with £7 million ($11.5 million) of equity and £53 million ($87.5 million) of borrowings, and concentrating on roots as well as fruits, is quite an achievement. (The Caradon story is described in Chapter 4.)

Magdalen Farm

Caradon had an extraordinarily successful share flotation in 1987, and for the first time in my life I possessed a significant amount of capital. But my elation soon turned to fretfulness. Why had such wealth come into my life? What was I meant to do with it? I was sure there was some higher purpose, but all my efforts could not reveal it. After three months, I realized I was less happy than before the flotation, so I got on with life and work as before, trusting that the answer would appear in its own time.

In May 1989 a vision emerged: an organic farm where people could learn how to align with natural principles and find sustainable fulfillment. I established an educational charity, the Wessex Foundation, as the framework, giving £1 million of my Caradon capital to fund it. In May 1990, I and the other trustees agreed to buy Magdalen Farm, a beautiful 130-acre farm in southwest England, on the Dorset–Somerset borders. Since

1990 it has changed from a rundown conventional farm to a pioneering organic farm and residential education center.

The focus of the Wessex Foundation is to promote learning about sustainability at all levels, including personal, social, business, and environmental sustainability. In ten years we have achieved a great deal, but we are not yet fully sustainable in any of these areas. The project has been instructive, satisfying, and difficult. The idea of creating an organic farm as a living basis for learning and sustainability has proved even more powerful than I had imagined. We don't have all the answers about working sustainably, but we are certainly learning.

From a starting point of complete ignorance, I learned about the practicalities of organic farming: finding and supporting the farm management, creating the business plans, and bringing the farm through the conversion phase and difficult early years. Magdalen has been an intense education for me, both personally and in the nature of management and leadership. Alongside this my consultancy and training work for organizations continued to develop, but for several years I saw no direct connection. This changed in 1997, when I learned the principles of environmental sustainability through The Natural Step process described in the Appendix.

Suddenly I saw how Magdalen Farm embodied these principles, and I realized that organic farming offers a powerful model for human sustainability at work. Developing this model has been the focus of my work since then. I have led workshops at Magdalen and elsewhere that have confirmed that people see the analogy clearly, and that it helps move them toward sustainability.

The Natural Advantage: Seven Principles of Organic Growth

The Natural Advantage model offers a process map for sustainable production. The first three principles, described in Chapters 2–5, deal with organic roots: creating the base conditions from which growth arises naturally, without being forced. The next two principles, covered in Chapters 6 and 7, are about organic growth: how to use sustainable inputs to achieve sustainable outputs. The last two principles, explored in Chapters 8 and 9, are about organic fruits: describing the characteristics of sustainable output, and how these evolve from organic inputs and processes.

The apple tree illustrated at the beginning of each chapter provides a good image for *The Natural Advantage*. Its roots provide the main inputs and the stable foundation for the whole structure of production. The trunk is like the growth processes, the central link between the roots and the fruits. And the apples are a good example of organic fruit: we can quickly tell the difference between real organic quality, an apple with satisfying taste, and a tasteless one, forcibly pushed to meet some nominal output standard.

As you might expect, the principles of *The Natural Advantage* are interlinked and interdependent: each requires and reinforces the others. The concept is also cyclical: the diversity and quality of outputs contribute to the roots and trunk of the process.

As you read this book, you will notice that it talks about the organic farmer as much as the farm. It is the combination of the two that creates a cultivated natural system. This has a parallel for you and your work. You could say that the farmer represents your awareness, your active intelligence, and your intent. The farm represents the other resources you bring to your work, such as intuition, practical skills, physical stamina, and feelings.

These all combine to form one living, productive organism, just as the farm and farmer operate together.

The seven principles are briefly outlined below.

1   *Ground condition*

To organic farmers, soil quality is the basis of sustainable output. They aim continually to improve the reserves and resilience of their soil while increasing its production. By contrast, forced farming progressively depletes and pollutes the soil, so that the output depends on ever-increasing amounts of external stimulants (fertilizer) and suppressants (pesticide).

This offers us ways to understand, improve, and sustain our own ground condition, our reserves and resilience. By cultivating our sources of fertility, our output at work grows naturally and sustainably.

2   *Natural energy*

The main energy sources for organic farms are sunlight, water, earth, air, and organic waste: natural, abundant, low cost and non polluting. Pushing output by control systems, deadlines, or supervisors is like using fossil fuels: it builds up residues that reduce natural resilience and fertility.

Recall times at work when you felt deeply appreciated, or highly inspired—remember how energized you felt, how the work flowed more easily. There are simple ways to stimulate and harness these energies that don't have polluting side effects.

3   *Composting waste*

The beauty of any natural cycle is that there is no waste: every output becomes the input to the next stage of the cycle. The waste in your work includes discarded energy and value—think about negative feelings, like anxiety, or subtle setbacks and conflicting data. Waste is usually messy: it takes new skills to collect and recycle it, but this can readily be done. Negativity can then become a source of fresh understanding and constructive energy.

Composting is a classic example of natural synergy: you get more out than you put in, and it provides a model of how to harness human energy waste in the workplace.

4 *Organic synergy: growing through uncertainty*

Organic farmers achieve results with less control and amid more uncertainty than people in any other job I know. They are great examples of how to achieve synergy through creative tension: using uncertainty, finding the "gift in the problem."

By combining our active intent and push with the skills of receptiveness and adaptability, we can create a natural process of dynamic growth that harnesses change to create output.

This co-creative approach is central to achieving results in conditions of change and uncertainty. Elements of co-creativity include tolerance for ambiguity, developing both intuition and logic, as well as synergy and assertiveness.

5 *Using natural growth cycles*

The organic approach does not "let nature take its course," but works *with* it. Organic farmers use natural cycles, such as crop rotation and the four seasons.

Applying this to your working situation, think of renewing your own energy by moving from a demanding task to an easy one, or from a structured to a fluid way of working. Or picture your work as part of a full cycle of seeding—growing—harvesting—rest.

6 *Resilience from diversity*

Even small organic farms have a diverse range of products or enterprises. This creates resilience: if one crop fails, or if demand drops, the overall business can sustain the blow. The various crops support each other and create synergy. Diversity is key to reducing weed and pest problems. So are wild margins, uncultivated land supporting the birds and insects that keep pests in check.

There are similar benefits at work. We can increase diversity in the way we work as well as in the range of tasks, and the wild margins for individuals and organizations make us more creative and adaptable to change.

7   *Real quality*

When you eat a piece of fruit, how do you judge its quality? Real quality is about taste, nutrition, and a feeling of satisfaction. Organic produce may look irregular, but it delivers real quality. Forced farming is geared to deliver only nominal quality in terms of size, appearance, consistency, and quantity.

An important feature of real quality is a deep, flexible, two-way relationship between producer and customer. The rapport and trust in such relationships are part of the satisfaction that the product delivers, and both parties are able to accept more change and uncertainty.

Many work situations push for nominal quality, but it's real quality that gives sustained satisfaction for the organization and its customers. Understanding the emotional value in your output, building direct and dynamic customer relationships, helping the organization to appreciate all this: these are ways toward sustaining high performance.

The Elusive Goal

Whether you work in a large organization, on your own, or somewhere in between, this book should be relevant to you. Whatever your work, you are probably finding that its demands, and the level of change and uncertainty, are more than you can easily handle. This book shows you how to go forward to meet these pressures constructively. We all have a natural capacity to grow sustainably and adaptably in our work. *The Natural Advantage* describes both the principles and the practicalities of cultivating this capacity.

The desire for sustainability is widespread, but understanding what it really means is elusive. The simple definition that I use is: *sustainability is meeting present needs without reducing future potential.* In whatever context this definition is applied, it probably raises many questions, but they are fruitful ones. Which needs and whose are they? Can all needs be met equally? Are needs different from wants or desires? What level of future potential are we trying to preserve and for how long? Do we want the future to be better than the present or not much worse? And on what criteria? These are massively complex but important questions. They are at least being explored with regard to the natural environment and material standards of living. Try relating these questions to your work and its sustainability for you personally.

The principles of sustainability apply at all scales and in all spheres: a farm, a region, the global ecosystem, and an individual, a team, an organization. As you understand and apply these principles in one area, you gain the potential to apply them in others.

One of the common misunderstandings I sense around sustainability is that it is a static state, a desirable but nebulous absence of nasty things. A sustainable condition is full of change, tension, and turbulence. The crucial difference from the culture in most workplaces, which seeks to control uncertainty and suppress conflict, is that these qualities are handled constructively and dynamically: there is flow as well as tension, synergy as well as conflict.

The move toward sustainability is not one frightening giant

leap: it's more a matter of progressing cyclically. With each repetition of the cycle, you move closer to true sustainability. The conversion period on a farm moving from forced to organic methods is often a tough time. It involves confusion as old dependencies are dropped and new methods are learned, partly by trial and error. Output may fall for a while, until the farm's natural vitality has had time to develop. You may face similar challenges in your own move to the organic way and these issues are covered in detail in Chapter 10. Going organic requires commitment, but the payback is excellent. It offers the prospect of deeper satisfaction, growing output value, and a way of working that renews you and meets change robustly.

As with many innovations, the move toward human sustainability at work is likely to be pioneered by individuals, small groups, and a handful of leading-edge businesses. Change in this area grows from the efforts of individuals, so this is the main application explored in this book. However, *The Natural Advantage* is also a blueprint for organizations, for both human and business sustainability: for example cultivating markets, developing them organically to create continuing sales, not exhausting their potential.

Before you decide to apply *The Natural Advantage* in your work, I suggest you read through the whole book. All seven principles are interdependent, and it's important to understand the whole model before you apply part of it. For example, in developing your ground condition and natural energy sources, it helps to have a picture of the diversity and quality of fruit you want to cultivate in your work.

Having read the whole book once, I suggest you then apply the principles in the order they are presented: starting with roots/inputs, moving on to growth processes, and finishing with fruits/outputs. Each chapter contains advice and relevant methods for applying the principles, illustrated with real-life examples drawn from my own experience, from participants in my workshops, and from business consultancy clients, although some names and details have been changed to protect confidentiality.

Sustainability check-in

The checklist below will help you make an initial assessment of how sustainable your current way of working is. For each question, give an intuitive rating between 0 and 10, and add up your scores. If your total score is over 60, your work is probably depleting you significantly.

---

a Ground condition
In relation to your work, how do you rate
your resources, your energy reserves?

10 Severely depleted
0 Abundant

Physical resources ☐
Emotional resources ☐
Mental resources ☐
Inspirational resources ☐

b Energy sources
Are the energy sources motivating your
work mostly forced, stressful and polluting,
or are they mostly natural, clean,
organic (e.g. enthusiasm)?

10 Highly stressful
0 Mostly natural

☐

c Composting waste
Do "waste issues" in your work (e.g. anxiety,
setbacks, conflict) accumulate and pollute your
energy, or do you recycle them as a source of
future growth?

10 Severe build-up
0 Totally recycled

☐

d Work processes
Do your ways of working mostly involve push
and stress: are they less flexible than the
demands on you? Can you combine active push
with receptive flow and find the synergy in
tension and uncertainty?

10 Fixed approaches,
low adaptability
0 Highly flexible,
synergistic

☐

e Using natural cycles
Is your work mostly linear, is output constant?
Do you use cycles, e.g. push–rest,
produce–review?

10 Constant push
0 Fully cyclical

☐

f Diversity
Is your work monotonous and repetitive?
Do you have enough diversity to give you
renewal and resilience?

10 Very monotonous
0 Diverse and renewing

☐

g Real quality
Are the results of your work truly satisfying
in quality for you and your clients, or not?

10 Mostly nominal
output, not fulfilling
0 Satisfying sense of
real quality for all parties

☐

2
Ground Condition: The Foundation

For the organic farmer, the earth is what you start with. Ground condition, soil quality, remains the barometer of the state of your productive system. Organic farmers know that soil is the powerhouse of their business. It may be the crops that earn the money, but the ground condition is the asset that creates them and supports future production. The earth is both a vital input and a vital process in producing the desired output. Ground in good condition literally manufactures fertility: from the life within it, from waste, and from the nutrients in the earth, air, and water.

The basic principle of ground condition is that you can only achieve results sustainably by cultivating the underlying fertility, the resources from which output grows naturally. This principle applies equally to crops and to people. The earth is a living organism which, treated organically, can renew its own potential and keep producing. A human being is a living organism too, and we can cultivate our productivity by the same principles. This contrasts with the approach in most work cultures and on conventional farms, where output depends on external pressures and ground condition is depleted, not renewed.

For me it has been inspiring to realize that the earth truly is a living system. Every square yard of organic earth teems with a variety of life that interacts to make it a productive, resilient organism. The US Department of Agriculture, in its definition of organic farming, says "the concept of the soil as a living system that develops the activities of beneficial organisms is central to this definition." Francis Blake in *Organic Farming and Growing* says "the number of micro-organisms (principally bacteria and fungi) in one small teaspoonful of soil is greater than the total number of people who have ever lived on this earth."

There are clear parallels between the earth and the human being as living organisms of extraordinary and effective complexity. To know and manage this complexity in detail is impossible and unnecessary, but if you cultivate a natural organism on the principles of sustainability, you don't need to manage all the details.

This may sound obvious, but it is quite different from the approach of the conventional farm or workplace. Here, a limited number of synthetic inputs are applied in mechanistic fashion to achieve desired outputs. Because most fertility in conventional systems comes from imported additives, not from the ground itself, the underlying resources are progressively diminished by misuse, and polluted by the residues of these synthetic inputs.

This has caused a crisis on many intensive farms, which have reached the stage of diminishing returns: crop yields are dropping, despite continued heavy use of artificial fertilizers; water pollution is severe; and the soil has little resilience to extreme

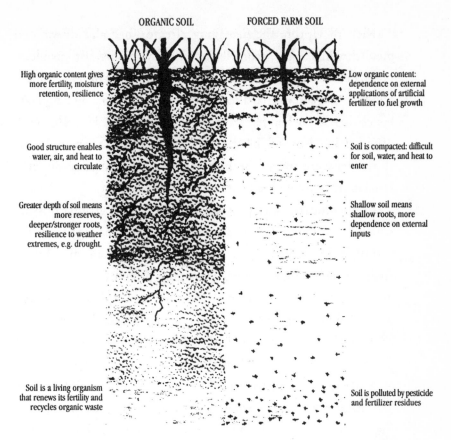

ORGANIC SOIL   FORCED FARM SOIL

High organic content gives more fertility, moisture retention, resilience

Low organic content: dependence on external applications of artificial fertilizer to fuel growth

Good structure enables water, air, and heat to circulate

Soil is compacted: difficult for soil, water, and heat to enter

Greater depth of soil means more reserves, deeper/stronger roots, resilience to weather extremes, e.g. drought.

Shallow soil means shallow roots, more dependence on external inputs

Soil is a living organism that renews its fertility and recycles organic waste

Soil is polluted by pesticide and fertilizer residues

Figure 1 Ground condition

weather and other new challenges, so the whole farm is vulnerable to change. The problems for human sustainability at work may be more subtle and less extreme, but they nevertheless exist.

Stephen Lessing

Stephen Lessing looked like a withered stick when I first met him: not what you'd expect from a 31-year-old high flyer, with an MBA from London Business School, already experienced in general management. I was the newly appointed marketing and sales director; Stephen, as marketing manager, was my potential number two.

Richard Upton, the managing director, had already warned me: "Stephen's got promise, but he's your biggest problem. He's demotivated, and I don't want it spreading." I liked Stephen, but he was hard to reach. It was in the body language: his chair was pushed hard against the back wall of his cluttered office, defensively facing the door; his head was at an angle, his shoulders were turned in, he rarely looked at anyone directly. His whole body seemed twisted, dry, airless, stiff.

Our company was part of a much larger group, Bessell, which had a reputation as a progressive, well-managed organization, but in reality it was more backward. I had joined with an impatient desire to be a managing director soon. All my military-hero circuits lit up at the sight of Stephen. I thought of El Alamein, the turning point in the North African campaigns of the Second World War. If I could break through with Stephen, I'd be in Tripoli within a week: I'd double my own effectiveness at a stroke. So I attempted to bounce him into action, smacking into him with the intensity of my will, painting the big picture, setting him tough deadlines, aiming to fire up his management reflexes. This all fell on barren ground: nothing took root.

I tried to spark him up with shared enthusiasm, dangling the carrot of our joint triumph and his prospects of succeeding me on my early promotion. He listened without response, as if this were some alien language, not the shared mythology of a fellow MBA. So I switched to the stick, telling him I wanted to get things moving fast, and I'd have to question his position if he couldn't respond. He seemed indifferent, as if he really wouldn't care if I fired him. Richard, my boss, was even more impatient than me. Within a fortnight he was jabbing at me for signs of progress. It was embarrassing: what kind of a whiz kid was I if I couldn't turn round someone of Stephen's talent?

Clearly, I was going wrong with Stephen. My methods were failing, so I had to think of things in a different way.

Cultivated Natural Systems

Think of a system, and what image comes up for you? For many people it's a manmade system: a computer, a fridge, an oil refinery. These are essentially mechanical systems, in which a specific input will consistently yield a predictable output: cause *A* leads to effect *B*. We're blessed with many of these systems, and they mostly give us predictable results with ever-higher reliability. But they mislead us about the way in which natural systems operate.

Think of a natural system, and what image do you get? Perhaps an ecosystem like a rainforest, or a weather system where elements are causally connected, but the outcomes are unpredictable and chaotic. Now ask yourself, what are the main differences between natural and mechanical systems?

Natural system
- ❖ Inputs are many, hard to define, measure or control.
- ❖ What happens inside the system (processes) is hard to specify and predict: it "has a life of its own."
- ❖ Outputs include states or qualities of being, as well as products or actions. Outputs are many, hard to control.

Mechanical system
- ❖ Inputs are readily defined and usually measured and controlled.
- ❖ What happens inside the system (processes) may be technically complex, but it is known and predictable.
- ❖ Outputs are mostly tangible, measurable. Inputs and processes are regulated to achieve specific desired outputs.

Are you a natural or a mechanical system? A human being is a natural system, but many of us treat ourselves like machines, and our culture promotes this. In my initial approach to Stephen Lessing, I was treating him as a mechanical system. I tried to use him like a machine, a tool, a vehicle to move me toward my output goals. It was only when my simplistic input–output mindset failed that I was forced to see Stephen as a person, and cultivate him as a natural system.

You may have a clear picture of some of the inputs you need for your own system, such as food, water, shelter. What about inputs directly relating to your work, to you as a productive system? Because we associate productive work with mechanical systems, we often expect ourselves to produce without inputs and maintenance. We don't have to make our own electricity, so why do we need to fuel our work? This is the issue that Stephen Covey describes as P/PC balance: the need to consider both production and production capacity.

Ecologists use three broad categories for ecosystems: developed, natural, and cultivated. Developed is essentially man-made, a town or suburban area. Natural is primarily wild, not intensively managed by people, such as moorland, marshland, or ancient forest. Cultivated means a natural habitat shaped and managed by people, for an economically productive purpose, typically farming. It is cultivated natural systems that offer the best model for people at work. Work is not just "letting nature take its course," leaving it in the wild. Nor is it centered on manmade resources. Work is centered on people: it involves taking nature as the basis, and working with it to achieve your aims. Cultivating ground condition is the foundation of this approach.

The Four Elements of Natural Growth

The concept of four elements—earth, air, fire, and water, which form the basis of all living matter—is an ancient one, found for example among the medieval alchemists. Whether we're considering a farm or a person, it is these four elements that interact to create fertile ground condition.

Earth

The soil is the growth medium: it provides the physical setting in which all the elements required for fertility combine. In people, the earth element relates to our physical body and physical energy.

Water

Water is essential to the whole process of growth. It carries nutrients from the earth via the root system to provide the material for the expansion of the plant. In human nature, water represents the emotional, feeling element. Too much or too little water stifles productivity. If we suppress all feelings in relation to our work, we are likely to be arid—uncreative and unable to relate fully and productively with others. Conversely, if we let ourselves be swamped by emotion, we are like waterlogged soil and the crops will rot. On the farm, physical soil structure, air circulation, and warmth enable water to play its role, and all this has analogies in the human field.

Air

Air is vital as an enabler and a fuel for growth. Ground in good condition has about 25 percent air content, and it is thanks to this that warmth and water can circulate and interact productively with the earth. The nitrogen in air also makes it an important source of fertility. Soil and plants breathe and need air to sustain life, just as we do. In human nature, air equates to inspiration, spiritual energy—the word inspiration literally means to breathe in.

Fire

The sun's heat is essential to maintain ground condition and generate plant growth. The fire element in the human system is mental energy: it's fast moving, fast changing, it can kindle and fuel growth, but can dry it up if taken to excess. For both people and farms, the fire element needs to be managed carefully: it has to be balanced with the other elements, and matched with crops that can use it well.

The four elements are explored in more depth in Chapter 4.

Learning From the Ecosystem

Figure 2 shows the composition of a typical organic soil, and highlights the importance of the air and water elements.

The earth element in the soil has two main components: mineral and organic matter. Although organic matter, humus, is only a few percent of the total, it is central to the soil's productivity. The humus promotes biological activity throughout the earth, and enables conversion of inert minerals into nutrients usable by the plant. It is also a key to soil structure, enabling the different elements to combine productively. I see the human equivalent of humus as vitality, or what the Chinese call *chi*, life energy. A person with high vitality has naturally high resilience and productivity, just like fertile ground.

The earth, water, and air elements combine with the fourth, heat, to form the soil ecosystem: a living organism that is both productive and self-renewing. To apply this analogy to human productivity, we don't need to go into the detail of how this

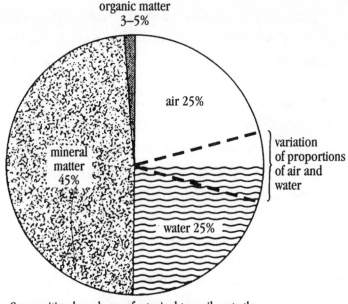

Composition by volume of a typical topsoil: note the surprisingly large proportion of air and water (although their exact proportions vary considerably), reflecting their importance as constituents of soil

Figure 2 *The organic system*

Reproduced with permission from *Organic Farming and Growing,* Francis Blake, Crowood Press.

ecosystem works. What is relevant for our purpose is to know the main features of good ground condition and how to cultivate them: these include soil structure, building fertility, and how to manage different soil types, which equate to different temperaments in human nature.

Soil types

The ground condition of any farm or garden is fundamentally shaped by its soil type, such as clay, chalk, or sand. Each soil type has characteristic strengths and problems and will suit some crops better than others. As The Natural Advantage process has evolved, I have developed a sense that the main soil types equate to temperament or personality types in people. Here is my summary of the main soil types and their human equivalents.

❖ *Sand*: sandy soils have an open texture and both water and organic matter tend to drain through them quickly. Basic fertility is low, but sandy soil can be highly productive if organic matter is regularly added. This equates to people who are potentially fiery and creative, but lack follow-through and stamina: they need frequent top-ups of fertility and good composting to avoid burnout. Stephen Lessing is an example of this soil type.

❖ *Silt*: this is the fine-textured, fertile earth found in river valleys. It is so fine that it lacks structure, and becomes clogged with water, too dense for air and warmth to circulate. A silty soil is like a person who is highly intelligent but impractical. An example of a silt temperament is Phil Morris, managing director of Alibi Publishing, profiled in the next chapter.

❖ *Clay*: a dense, heavy soil, which can easily become waterlogged or hard and dry. Its inherent fertility is fair, but can be developed through cultivation, drainage, and adding humus. In people, this equates to a temperament that is rather serious, and has difficulty in handling emotions, such as Alison Martin, whom you will meet later in this chapter.

❖ *Loam*: a mixture of the three soil types above. These combination soils mostly have better structure and fertility than the single soil types. Although they can be highly productive, they still need considerable care and cultivation. The human equivalent is a temperament that is more complex, more versatile, and more productive.

❖ *Chalk*: on a chalky subsoil the topsoil is thin and alkaline, which limits the range of plants it can support. Chalk soils tend to dryness, because water drains through them. Their fertility is fair, but can be developed by adding organic matter. A person with a chalk temperament may be a maverick, with a risk of seeming dry, sour, and unemotional. An example of this type is Salim Hussain, whose story is told in Chapters 5 and 7.

❖ *Peat*: peat soils have high organic content and good structure; they retain moisture, but also drain well. However, peat is highly acid, which stifles biological activity and means that left to itself, peat soil is usually quite dead and unproductive. Someone with a peat temperament is usually intelligent and talented, but risks being bitter, disaffected, unable to apply their potential to their work.

Using soil types as a model for different human characters offers another simple and revealing way to understand both the needs and the potential of your ground condition. In farming, it is clear that some crops will thrive on one soil type and fail on another. As you explore your own soil type, consider whether your work outputs suit it, and whether you have a balance between crops that are demanding and those that are restorative for your temperament.

You don't just add water

With Stephen Lessing, my intuition told me that this was a deep problem, that it was almost insulting Stephen to try the quick-fix methods I began with. I sensed he had a genius for implementation that would complement my passion for big ideas, so I persisted. He was like a formerly fertile soil after years of drought: you don't just add water, you have to recondition the whole ground structure. If an organic farmer wanted to grow wheat on a field four years in a row, his friends would urge him not to. They'd know that the crop yield would be poor and the soil would be exhausted. This is what happened to Stephen. In his previous company he drove himself hard throughout his twenties, and at 28 was invited to step up from marketing manager to general manager. It was a business with a great brand name, but a mess in every other respect.

Stephen grabbed at a chance that was too much, too soon for him. Within a year he had gone from fired up to burned out. Neither he nor the business performed well, and he left bitter, depleted, with his self-confidence withered. Moving to marketing manager with a larger company looked a sensible sideways step, a semi-fallow season to renew his fertility—but it turned out to be another setback. My predecessor had become disillusioned with the whole business world, and dumped his cynicism on Stephen like acid rain during the year before he left. Stephen had hoped he would succeed him, but knew he was in no condition to do so: he was dried up, as barren as baked mud.

After several weeks of getting more and more wound up, I had to accept that my irresistible force had met an immovable object. I couldn't impose the effect I wanted so I turned my raw, impatient energy to the salesforce, where there were some quick wins that kept the boss off my back. I still had a clear vision of how Stephen could be, but no sense of how to make it happen.

Recovery cycle

I used to seek Stephen out at the end of the afternoon and sit in his office, telling him about my ideas and enthusiasms, hoping that my own inspiration would gradually revive him, breathe some air into him. I also made a point of appreciating him: for what he was, for qualities like clarity and straight talking, not for achievement. I sensed that if I tried to force output from him, Stephen would close up completely; whereas if he felt warmly valued, with no instant return expected, he would start to open up like a field ready for sowing. Gradually, trust and empathy developed between us.

A few months later, Stephen and I were working very well together. We had a direct and effective dialogue: he shaped and sparked my ideas, and I did the same for his implementation. He had forced me to learn a principle that I apply now in any working relationship, even with seemingly biddable people: I don't get sustainable results or the full picture by imposing my will, I need to leave space to hear the other person and collaborate.

After a year of working together, I appointed Stephen as one of three regional managers responsible for a salesforce of 80 people. He was cerebral in his approach and marketing work had reinforced this. Sales management drew him into the feeling side of his nature, as well as the physical, practical side. This is the same principle as developing qualities in the soil by the crops you grow on it. A year later I was promoted, and Stephen succeeded me. He did well as marketing and sales director, and was later promoted to a managing director position.

Although I wasn't using The Natural Advantage model when I worked with Stephen Lessing, it fits with the successful approach I evolved. When we first met, his ground condition was very poor. His organic content, i.e. his creativity, motivation, and initiative, was low. His soil depth was good, so his potential was high, but the soil structure was awful, what a farmer would call compacted. When a soil is compacted, it has been squashed down, there is little air content, it has no openness, so the ingredients for growth can't get in. It takes time, patience, and persistent effort to help closed ground to open up, as I eventually realized.

With Stephen, I took off the pressure for big thinking and a high level of output. Letting him work on the smaller issues was like growing a restorative, undemanding crop on the field. Spending time hanging out with him was like using an aerating roller to open up the soil. Gradually he started to absorb appreciation and inspiration, like sunlight and air, and the momentum and vitality of his natural system revived. I would say that Stephen's soil type, like mine, is basically sandy. His inherent reserves are low, but he can be highly productive given good inputs of fertility. When he and I started working well together, we developed habits that raised both our fertility and our output.

Stephen's main assets were his physical and mental energy, which equate to the earth and fire elements, but his approach left him physically drained, like earth whose fertility is exhausted. And his over-use of fiery, mental energy left him dried up and burned out. If you push a person, or a field, to produce a demanding crop for several years using unsustainable methods, their resources will be depleted and polluted. Stephen's ambition had drawn him to a high-pressure job in a struggling company: you could say he gave it everything he'd got, but he did so in a way that ignored renewal completely. Sustainable growth needs to draw on all four elements: earth, water, fire, and air.

Alison Martin

I met Alison Martin on one of my workshops at Magdalen Farm on how to fulfill yourself sustainably in work. When she spoke about why she'd come on the program, she said: "I'm not at a crossroads, I'm at the end of the road, suicidal. I'm sick of my work, and propping myself up with anti-depressants, cigarettes and wine. I feel like my job is killing me." Alison was 40 years old, a successful middle manager in a high-pressure job in the National Health Service. But her skin was sallow and she wore a tense, negative expression. In ground condition terms, I felt she was a clay type, waterlogged, bogged down, swamped by negative feelings.

As the weekend went on, Alison reached the same view as me of her ground condition. She questioned Peter Norman, the farm manager, about the boggy field at the west end of the farm and how he was dealing with it. "The land there is clay," Peter explained, "so it's got a tendency to waterlogging, but we can improve it over time. The main structural change is drainage: we're putting a network of field drains in to draw off the excess water. Another thing we do is turn the pigs on to it."

I could see Alison wince at this. We were standing by the field and it looked a complete mess: a chaos of mud, with vast sows wallowing in it, grunting happily. Peter grinned at her. "Sometimes in farming, when you've got a bit of a mess, the way through is to make a complete mess of it. What the pigs do is churn the clay up really deep, so you get more organic matter mixed down into the soil. They open up the structure, so the air gets in. Wet clay is awful for persistent weeds like docks, but the pigs root them out. We also add light compost, like vegetable waste, which breaks down into humus and makes the soil less dense."

Soon after this Alison came over to me. "Alan, I'm really excited by all this: I can see there's something here for me, but I can't make it out yet." She shook her head crossly. "It's ridiculous: I don't know anything about this farming stuff."

"You don't need to be a farmer to work this out," I said. "It's about you. Start with putting your attention fully into your body, and feel how it's in a similar condition to the field. The water saturating that clay is like negative feelings bogged down within your physical self."

There was a tense pause. "OK," she began slowly. "This is old feelings in me that have been down there for years: rejection, self-dislike, depression. And it feels really stuck, sticky like clay. It's awful, it's literally like a bog. These are stagnant emotions, there's nowhere for them to go."

We stood silently for a while, as the pigs grunted on around us. Eventually she looked up: "But on a farm if you've got a bog or a muddy field, you take an overview, you look at the contours, where the land slopes, and how to channel the water."

Alison thought further, and smiled. "Yes. I am quite capable of mapping out these stuck feelings, and figuring out how to move them. It's like engineering for feelings, isn't it?"

"Brilliant," I said. "That's exactly it. It's using your mind to create the channels and direction by which the feelings can move, and as they flow, they become clear and useful, like the difference between stagnant and running water."

Although Alison thought she already knew her story, the causes of the stuck feelings, it felt quite different when she mapped them, spelling out the whole sequence of relevant events through her life. Doing this harnessed her brainpower, her problem-solving talents, which up to now had had no way of engaging with her emotional stagnation.

Send in the pigs

A few weeks later, Alison phoned me. "I've figured out the pigs," she said proudly.

"Tell me."

"Well, I remembered how you took me through the drainage thing, and I applied the same method. I got back into that connection between my physical self and that muddy field, and then imagined what the pigs would mean for me. My first reaction was, I felt like screaming. It was an invasion: they were going even deeper into the crap, opening the soil up, exposing everything, churning it over."

"So what did that mean for your situation?" I asked.

"It said that mapping the territory was only a start: I had to let myself express these feelings, take the risk of being really churned up. That'd be far better than staying stuck in them. So I've arranged some counseling sessions, and it's incredible how much lighter I feel for letting this stuff out."

Alison needed to be "lost enough to find herself," as Robert Frost so aptly put it. Part of her story dealt with her parents, who insisted that girls should always be smiling, sweet, and subservient. By now, she could see that water was useful when moving and a problem when stagnant: she began to express her feelings at work, instead of bottling them up. The ground condition model gave her a new and on-going approach to managing her feelings, using her mental power, and handling surprises with resilience. As she put it, "Whatever comes up, if I take it back to my ground condition, I get a simple sense of what to do."

Alison's experience is typical of many people who have used The Natural Advantage process: making the link between ground condition in the soil and in your own nature can yield new understanding and resolution, even for deep-rooted issues. Most of us have some sense of affinity with the soil, and the ground condition model has an evocative power to show us what it means to work as a natural system. With practice it becomes quick and easy to assess your ground condition, and to form a clear view of what you need to renew it.

3
Cultivating Ground Condition

There is a saying that "the best way to learn fast is to make a lot of mistakes in a short space of time." My own learning about ground condition started in earnest when I worked my way into health problems in 1994.

From 1976 to 1990, I was continuously involved in senior management positions, most of them turnarounds. A 60- to 80-hour week was my norm, and I felt the stresses of these jobs intensely. Yet my health was excellent. Although I was not consciously managing my ground condition, I did so intuitively. Looking back, many elements of good ground maintenance are apparent.

For a start, there was a sound rotation cycle in my work and non-work activities. Every job involved managing large teams, so I had a range of contacts. This rotated with intense work on individual tasks. I was also traveling a lot, and long hours on planes and trains were my recovery cycle: time to relax and to reflect and digest the long hours of continuous output. My children were young during these years, and my family life was absorbing and satisfying, forming another part of the renewal cycle.

I was also acutely aware that working these hours would wreck me unless I maintained my physical health. Frequent exercise was a priority. I was careful about diet and alcohol. A strong sense of purpose and inspiration in each job kept my energy renewed. I had a vision of what I wanted to achieve for the businesses and the people in them. I was also clear and positive about my own career goals, both fulfillment and future progression.

In 1994, my context was very different. There was no business structure, no boss, no budget, no job description. I was working alone and with a small group of people at one location, Magdalen Farm. My kids were engrossed in friends, not family, so I had lost that counterbalance. I became emotionally tied up with the short-term problems of the project. My vision and perspective were overwhelmed by a sense of having to scrabble for survival. So I became hooked on driving for results, pushing the crop, not feeding the soil, in myself or the rest of the team.

Although my working hours were now easier, I was not maintaining my condition and my physical resources became exhausted. I was swamped, waterlogged by the emotional reactions that the project and the people brought up in me: intense anger, fear, and bewilderment. All my mental firepower, which had worked well in large businesses, seemed irrelevant in this chaos. But then, growth stops in sodden soil because the warmth and air can't circulate.

In 1994, when I fell ill with candida, I realized I had to take my health seriously. In ground condition terms, candida is a sign that humus and biological activity are low, that the natural system has lost its resilience to new challenges. From this crisis,

I developed a strong interest in what I called personal energy management. My approach built on books like Stephen Covey's *Seven Habits of Highly Effective People*. He writes of four types of human energy: physical, emotional, mental, and spiritual. I developed a detailed set of methods to manage these four energies.

In hindsight, I can see that in the 1980s I used the routines of the job, the needs of my children, and my liking for fixed habits to create a style for my work and life that was sustainable, but in fact quite rigid. It was outside in, not principle based. Nowadays, my work has few routines and is largely self-directed. I have grown my approach outward from the principles. Although I still have episodes of fatigue, my work style is now largely sustainable and pretty resilient to changes.

Developing Fertility

Most individuals and organizations are preoccupied with the crop, the outcome of their work. It's as if we are so overwhelmed by short-term economic pressures that we can't step back and balance the equation between roots and fruits. The principle of sustaining ground condition in organic farming points to the basis for human sustainability at work. It fits the basic principle set down by Eve Balfour, one of the pioneers of organic farming in Britain: "Feed the soil, and the soil will feed the plant." If we focus solely on feeding the crop, we lose the capacity to create a different output, to overcome unexpected problems.

One of the important features of fertile ground condition is structure (see Figure 3). Good structure is permeable, so that air, heat, and water can get into the soil and excess water can drain through it. It has enough openness that roots can penetrate deep down into it, and enough strength to support the root structures firmly.

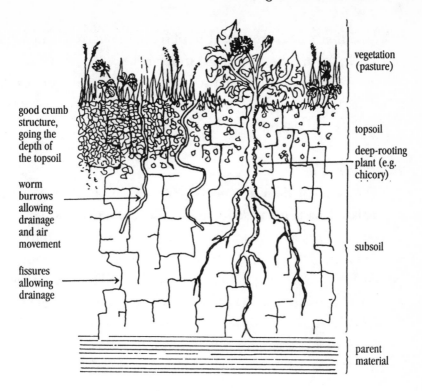

good crumb
structure,
going the
depth of
the topsoil

worm
burrows
allowing
drainage
and air
movement

fissures
allowing
drainage

vegetation
(pasture)

topsoil

deep-rooting
plant (e.g.
chicory)

subsoil

parent
material

Figure 3 Cross-section of healthy soil

Reproduced with permission from *Organic Farming and Growing,* Francis Blake,
Crowood Press

The figure also shows the importance of depth. The most
fertile part of the soil is the topsoil: the layer that contains
humus, organic matter. The depth of topsoil is a measure of
how much available fertility the soil has, of its capacity to
absorb more organic matter, and of its resilience. For example,
a deeper layer of topsoil can support plants longer in a drought.
The usable depth of soil is greater on organic farms, and the cultivation methods mean that plants can also access moisture and
nutrients from the subsoil.

One of the beauties of natural systems is symbiosis, the
association of two organisms that contribute to each other's
support. The two basic issues to consider in managing ground

condition are structure and fertility, and there is a symbiotic link between them. Improving structure helps the earth's capacity to produce fertility and supply it to a crop; and actions to raise fertility will develop soil structure, the texture and resilience of the soil.

Building structure

The most common structural problem with soil is compaction. This means that the soil is too dense: air, water, and warmth cannot circulate. This inhibits the biological activity in the earth and hence fertility drops. It is more difficult for plant roots to penetrate compacted soil, as well as less rewarding because there are fewer nutrients. These problems are worse on intensive farms: conventional farmers feed the plant, not the soil, and do not concern themselves with soil structure. Fertility is added at the surface, which encourages plants to develop shallow root systems, instead of building structure by rooting deeply.

Relating this to human ground condition, compaction is one of the commonest problems I see in people at work. Because output is forced by artificial pressures at the surface, it is shallow rooted. There is a lack of air in the soil: a lack of real inspiration in the work. As a result of this, the water element—feelings about work—cannot circulate. You can see an example of this in the case of Stephen Lessing in the previous chapter.

One of the ways an organic farmer cures compaction is by planting crops that will do the job for him. Vigorous, deep-rooting plants can penetrate compacted soil, opening up the structure and unlocking its fertility; an example is the chicory plant in Figure 3. Another method of improving structure is mechanical cultivation. Magdalen has 50 acres of permanent pasture, silty soil alongside the River Axe, which cannot be plowed because these fields are liable to flooding that would wash away the topsoil. Silty soils are fine textured and prone to compaction, so a spiked roller towed behind a tractor was used to open up the soil to let in more air and increase its productivity. A third method is to use the weather. Heavy clay soils are very prone to compaction, but over time this can be broken down by simple weathering—a repeated succession of wetting and drying, freezing and thawing.

All three methods to renew compacted soil have parallels in human ground condition. Growing a restorative, undemanding crop on a field is like letting a person rebuild their confidence and vitality gradually, working on smaller projects that restore a sense of capability and harness all four elements. Using mechanical cultivation to open up the soil structure is equivalent to a variety of deliberate interventions to bring more air, more inspiration, to a person or team. These can include team building or visioning processes, or the more informal approach I took with Stephen. Using the weather to break compacted soil down is like a person encountering situations that confront them with their condition and force them to change. The pressures of Alison Martin's job combined with the visit to Magdalen Farm to bring her to the point of seeking a different way.

The other common structural problem is waterlogging. Heavy clays in particular are liable to retain too much water, so air circulation and biological activity are suppressed. One solution is field drains, a network of pipes that will remove some of the water content and channel it elsewhere. Adding organic matter to lighten the soil will also help, as can crops or mechanical cultivation. Alison Martin is an example of how this applies to human ground condition. Her decision to open up old, stagnant feelings, and get counseling help to process them, is like recycling rotting waste into fertile organic matter that can lighten the soil.

Building fertility

Developing fertility is the second main aspect of cultivating good ground condition. In organic farming, crop choice and rotation cycles play a central role in this. At Magdalen Farm, several fields were exhausted from producing demanding crops like cereals and potatoes for too long. These fields were reseeded as clover leys, pasture kept for a few years as part of a longer rotation. Nitrogen is the most important nutrient required for plant growth and demanding crops consume a lot of it. What is remarkable about clover is that it actually draws nitrogen from the atmosphere and fixes it in the soil through its root system. The seed mix for these clover leys included deep-rooting herbs like chicory, so that the crop improved soil structure as well as fertility.

Fertility can also be developed through manure and compost. The growth potential in waste products is harnessed and applied where it is most needed. Although organic farmers prefer to avoid importing fertility, this is sometimes necessary, especially in the early years. Organic manure can be brought in to speed up the renewal process. Organic standards also permit some use of natural additives to correct mineral deficiencies, for example seaweed, lime, or rock phosphate. These are quite different in function from artificial fertilizers. It's like the difference between a vitamin supplement and a pep pill. Additives on organic farms are designed to work gradually to improve ground condition, not to act directly on the plant in the kickstart method of artificial fertilizers.

How does this relate to human ground condition? It highlights a basic principle of sustainable productivity at work: cultivating underlying fertility, not depending on external spot applications to force a particular crop. By doing so, you create resources in yourself that are both adaptable and self-renewing. Human ground condition, like healthy soil, has innate vitality to meet the unexpected and produce growth despite a variety of problems. The methods of achieving this draw on several of the other principles of The Natural Advantage, explained in the following chapters.

Ground condition dipstick

Consider how the ground condition model applies to you personally. How is your soil structure—do you combine openness and strength? Do you feel that your topsoil, your fertile layer, is deep or shallow? What soil type do you think you are, and how does this suggest you can build your own fertility? How high is your humus content, the vitality that is a catalyst for growth?

Figure 4 provides a quick way to check one of the most important aspects of ground condition, the balance of the four growth elements.

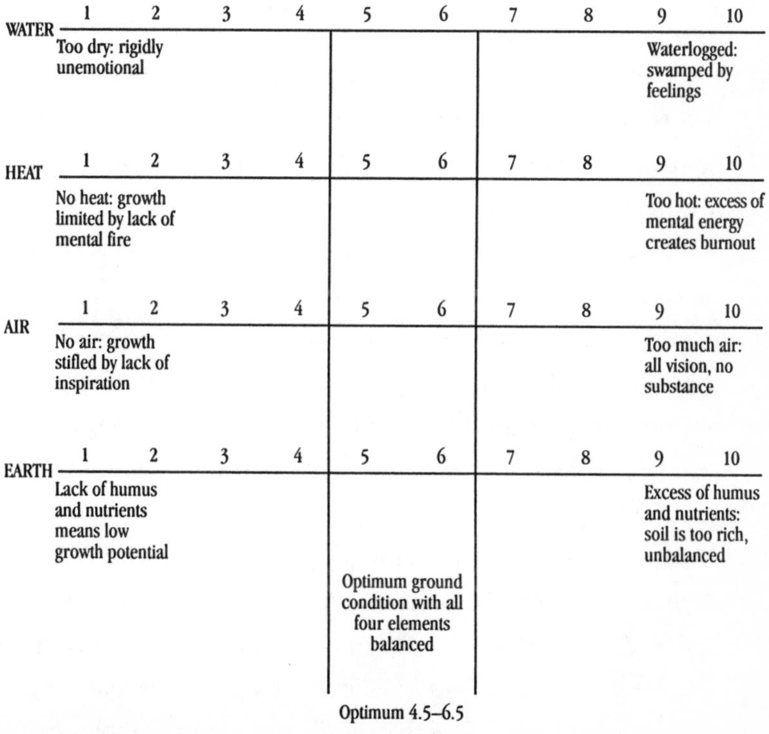
WATER
1 2 3 4 5 6 7 8 9 10
Too dry: rigidly unemotional
Waterlogged: swamped by feelings
HEAT
1 2 3 4 5 6 7 8 9 10
No heat: growth limited by lack of mental fire
Too hot: excess of mental energy creates burnout
AIR
1 2 3 4 5 6 7 8 9 10
No air: growth stifled by lack of inspiration
Too much air: all vision, no substance
EARTH
1 2 3 4 5 6 7 8 9 10
Lack of humus and nutrients means low growth potential
Excess of humus and nutrients: soil is too rich, unbalanced
Optimum ground condition with all four elements balanced
Optimum 4.5–6.5

Figure 4 Ground condition dipstick

Ground Condition in Organizations

The ground condition concept works for teams and whole organizations as well as individuals. While soil types and condition will be more diverse in a group, there will also be a collective ground condition that usually reflects that of the group leader. The managing director's outlook shapes the ground condition of the whole company. When I worked for Richard Upton his approach was to apply intense pressure for current-year results, and to cut short debate on obstacles or future implications. This was like an intensive farmer relying on heavy use of fertilizer and pesticide to push the crop. His approach delivered high profits for several years, but led to deep, underlying problems that emerged some years later.

Although it is harder, it is quite possible for an individual or team to work sustainably within an overall culture that is depleting the ground condition. The key to this is to operate according to dual standards. Provided that you meet the output demands, you can usually do it your own way if you get on with it quietly.

A few progressive companies already monitor and manage aspects of ground condition. For example, BP and Glaxo run regular staff attitude studies that include some questions in these areas. The concept of the learning company has parallels with the ground condition model: the methods applied in developing learning organizations are relevant to creating productive ground condition.

Improving the quality of working life can be acknowledged as desirable, but won't of itself get the issue on to a company's action agenda. However, there are now numerous examples of businesses that have improved performance by humanizing their culture. One such is Wyeth, a leading international pharmaceuticals supplier. Between 1994 and 1997, Wyeth implemented a major program of training and process development with the aim of increasing effectiveness and the capacity to handle change. The framework for this program has been Investors In People, a scheme endorsed and supported by the UK government. One important feature has been training in interpersonal skills, which has enabled a deeper level of personal involvement and collaboration. These have included assertiveness, influencing skills, and conflict resolution. The principle that each individual has primary responsibility for their personal development and learning has been firmly established; this is achieved by annual reviews with line managers to agree a personal development plan for each individual.

Stephen Isherwood, Wyeth's company training and development manager, says: "We have seen many benefits in both business performance and personal effectiveness as a result of our Investors In People program. Continuous change and learning are now accepted as the norm. Development objectives are agreed between the participant and their manager before attending a training course. Afterwards the ability of the participant to deliver enhanced performance and the agreed objective is reviewed and evaluated. The results from this support my view that the steps we have taken at Wyeth to humanize our culture and increase personal involvement have contributed significantly to our business performance."

Alibi Publishing

When Working Vision was asked to facilitate a culture change program for Alibi in 1998, I could see that this assignment would be both exciting and dangerous. Alibi was a profitable, expanding company of 150 people, publishing several specialist magazines for the information technology sector. The firm was dominated by Phil Morris, a forthright but likable accountant.

He had been brought in as a troubleshooting managing director in 1995, at the age of 33. As Phil put it, "I've turned a blooming shambles into a winner, and I know it's down to me. I've got a smashing team here. They'll do anything I tell them, but that's the point: till now, I've done all the thinking and telling."

Phil had a sharp mind, good judgment, and terrific vitality, so his dominating, directive style had produced results. However, in ground condition terms his approach was disastrous. The entire organization depended on him for the inputs to generate the outputs, and everyone knew it. As one of the directors put it to me, "Just occasionally, Phil asks us what we think. He hardly waits for a reply, and we know it's not worth bothering. He'll have thought it through better than we ever could."

Phil had been asked by Alibi's German parent to focus on overseas acquisitions and development. His brief to us was: "Develop my guys so they can run this business sustainably without me."

My colleagues and I began with a detailed check on ground condition: individual interviews with Phil, his 11 direct subordinates, and a sample of people at other levels. Just as the soil on conventional farms becomes lazy and inactive because fertility is applied at the surface, so too with Alibi. The soil structure was compacted, with little air or water: no inspiration or feeling in the people. The level of humus and biological activity, the vitality and initiative, was low.

We diagnosed the soil type for Phil and the overall company as silty. Phil himself had a strong vision for the business and intense personal ambition. These created air within his soil to make him highly fertile. However, the rest of the organization had the typical problems of silty soil: poor structure, low air content, and low productivity, despite high potential. We designed a mix of workshops and individual coaching for Phil and his management team. A crucial part of this was running sessions for the group without Phil, so that they could develop their own ground condition and ease out of their dependence on him.

Until then, disputes between members of the team had always been resolved via Phil. Gradually we encouraged each individual and the whole group to develop their own vision and purpose for the business, and a sense of their ability to pursue these. This was effectively opening up the soil structure and letting air and inspiration in. We coached the team to start voicing issues directly to each other, and trained them in such skills as assertiveness and conflict resolution. They began to acquire a mental toolkit to handle their feelings effectively. The process also developed the structure of their ground condition, building a combination of openness and strength. Through a live-action simulation and a forum session on their current business issues, we built the team's ability to look at problems and conflicts, and use them constructively. They learned to compost their waste, which meant that the humus level and biological activity improved for the group and for individuals (there is more on composting in Chapter 5).

Our initial summary of the atmosphere at Alibi was banter culture: it was arid, cerebral, devoid of feeling. We sensed that Phil and several of the directors didn't know how to handle emotions. Another step in improving ground condition was to introduce moisture, the feeling element, into the culture. We began by developing the mental abilities to handle emotions, like channels for water. Then we used a series of experiential exercises, including some physical activities involving risk and trust. Gradually, the loud ones who used humor to avoid emotion became quieter, and the silent ones started to voice their feelings. We knew we had crossed a watershed when the loud ones themselves started to open up about their areas of vulnerability.

This program produced a lasting change in the ground condition at Alibi. The biggest problem, as I had feared, was Phil himself. Whenever short-term performance wobbled, he reverted to directive mode. It took several stormy run-ins between him and me in front of his team before he learned the art of constructive conflict. Phil told me: "You've earned your brass, lad, having your head bitten off and coming back for more. But I've got the drift: it's about finding solutions, not winning debates."

Ground Condition in Daily Practice

The key to achieving sustainability is to take its principles to heart, so that they shape your daily activities from the inside out. Setting outside-in targets and adopting techniques, vowing to check your ground condition every morning, may help you break bad habits, but is not of itself sustainable. The best way to take these principles to heart is to keep using them: play with them, try them out in real-life situations, your own and the organization's, until you have experienced how they work. In this way, they create natural structure, they become part of your own living system. Remember that all seven principles of *The Natural Advantage* are interdependent and mutually reinforcing. Trying to cultivate your ground condition without enabling it through the other six principles will not get you far.

The Chinese believe in taking medicine when you're healthy—the idea is to avoid getting ill in the first place. In the same way, the ground condition principle works well as preventive maintenance, sustaining fertility at high levels. The model also offers a clear blueprint for recovering vitality, but remember that this will need to be maintained. Ground condition is more than simple fitness. The specific aspects of soil quality can give you tailored guidance on addressing your own particular situation. If you get lost, go back to the analogy. Imagine yourself as a piece of ground and see what your soil condition is calling for. Once you have read the whole book, you should find that the other principles enable you to resolve your current need in a sustainable way.

It is important to see the limitations and the strengths of the organic farming model. A person is more like a farm than a field: capable of producing several crops, on different cycles, in parallel. The living earth has an intelligence and adaptability that echo the human, but on a lesser scale. The level of conscious intelligence, will, and change potential in people and organizations is immense: it exceeds the scope of any model.

Good structure is essential in accessing the soil's fertility, and the same is true for people at work. In the human context, good structure means cultivating a combination of openness and strength, and ensuring that the elements required for growth are both present and accessible. The other main element in good ground condition is fertility. While humus, organic matter, is only 3–5 percent of typical soil content, a small change in this level has a major impact on both the resourcefulness and the output of the soil. This is a valuable pointer for each of us, and for organizations. While the juice, the life energy, may appear to be a small part of the whole picture, its importance as a catalyst deserves great attention. Fertility also requires the presence, in balanced proportions, of the four growth elements. The implications of this for people at work are explored further in the next chapter.

4
Natural
Energy

If we ask what makes the conventional farm or workplace unsustainable, a prime factor is its use of unnatural, forced energy sources. Factory farming takes most of its energy from non-renewable sources, fossil fuels, and minerals, whose residues pollute the earth and groundwater. Consider the parallel in the workplace: Where does your personal energy come from? Often, work output is fueled by stress, fear, or pressure.

In both cases, forced energy stimulates the problems as much as the desired crop: it reduces the natural capacity for self-renewal, pollutes the outputs, and saps the underlying resources. The organic way is less controllable, and may be more labor intensive, but it yields better-quality crops and renews the means of production.

This second principle of *The Natural Advantage* grows directly from the first. Natural energy inputs are essential both to create good ground condition and to use it. In this chapter, we move on from the underlying conditions for growth to the energy inputs that create the desired output.

Our basic model for translating the natural energy principle from organic farming to the workplace will be the four elements introduced in Chapter 2: earth, water, fire, and air. Considering these four elements in plant growth provides quite specific pointers on cultivating natural energy productivity in our work. In the same way, intensive farming methods show how conventional workplace cultures diminish natural vitality, and raise dependence on forced energy inputs to achieve results. A fuller exploration of natural energy principles is given in the Appendix: The Natural Step.

Feeding the problems

During the workshop at Magdalen Farm that Alison Martin attended, she got into a lively discussion about energy and farming with Peter Norman, the farm manager. Alison attacked the question head on.

"Peter, I can't see what's wrong with putting fertilizer on your crops. Surely it's just like having a bit of sugar on your breakfast cereal? I mean, it's just an energy boost, giving nature a helping hand."

Peter smiled and shook his head. "No, it's more like having a bowl full of sugar and nothing else. How would that feel?"

Alison, Peter, and I had taken a stroll after lunch. It was a sultry June day, and we were leaning on a gate, looking at the roll of hills down to the River Axe and up the other side into Somerset.

Alison gave Peter an intimidating stare. "Stop exaggerating, it can't be that bad."

"Artificial fertilizers don't give nature a helping hand, they kick it out the door. After a few years, you're completely dependent on importing energy to get the growth."

Alison frowned. "But that's like Britain importing its timber because we can't grow enough here. It might not be ideal, but it's not the end of the world."

Peter was getting quite excited by now. "It's nothing like imported timber! If your growth depends on artificial fertilizers, you're creating all sorts of knock-on problems and an inferior crop. Look, why don't I show you?"

Peter led us down the lane, across a cattle grid, on to Rookery Farm, adjacent to Magdalen. "What we've got here," he said, "is a 30-acre field of intensively farmed wheat. Come and see, I'll show you what's really happening."

At first glance, things didn't look so different from next door. Alison stared at the wheat around her. "These plants are going on fine. What's the problem?"

Peter snorted. "The captain of a Roman galley might say the same. But it's hardly sustainable, is it? Have a look here."

Alison knelt beside him and looked closely. "Ugh! Some kind of tiny insect, lots of them, crawling all over the plant."

"They're aphids," Peter explained. "The nitrogen fertilizer they put on this crop is like an overdose of artificial energy. It kick-starts the plants but it also kick-starts the problems. Like these aphids. They suck the sap from the wheat, they encourage fungi, and they carry viruses."

"But you could sort this out with a pesticide, surely?" Alison said.

Peter laughed wryly. "Sure, and that's what they do here: we're only seeing aphids because we're up in the corner where the spray can't reach. At Magdalen Farm, we have a lot of ladybirds and ground beetles that eat the aphids. The pesticides here kill the predators as well as the pests."

We stood silently, taking it in. "And here's another problem," Peter said. "What do you see between the rows of potato plants?"

"Well," said Alison, "there's a lot of weeds growing in this corner, and there's dead weeds all over the main part of the field."

Peter nodded. "One of the problems with nitrates is they make everything grow. In fact, the weeds grow faster than the plants, because they're good at using whatever energy is around. This guy's weed problems are much worse than Magdalen's. So he has to dose his land with herbicide and pesticide. If you try to quick-fix your first problem, you just get into deeper trouble."

"And I suppose he'd get resistant strains of weeds, just as he would with the insect pests?" Alison asked.

"Exactly."

Dirty energy, diminishing returns

Alison stood up, dusting herself off gingerly. "OK, Peter, I'm getting the picture and it's pretty grim. But if fertilizers are part of the dirty energy problem, where does your clean energy come from?"

"In any sustainable system, energy use is crucial. Right?"

Alison nodded impatiently. "Sure."

"So what do you think a sustainable approach would look like?"

Alison thought for a minute. "I guess you'd use renewable energy sources. You'd recycle energy, and you'd minimize usage."

Peter smiled. "That's exactly what organic farmers do and this guy's the complete opposite. The raw material for his fertilizers, herbicides, and pesticides is basically fossil fuel. Plus you've got the energy used in processing, transporting, and spreading the stuff. So the main energy he uses for his outputs here is imported, it's dirty, polluting, and it's in an unnatural form."

"How do you mean?"

"I mean it's not compatible with natural systems."

"Feed the soil, and the soil will feed the plants?" Alison asked.

"Yes. These artificial fertilizers are soluble chemicals: it's like giving a human being a massive intravenous dose of one growth nutrient. What would happen if you got all your food that way?"

Alison shuddered. "I guess my digestive system would just stop working."

"Exactly." Peter gestured at the field. "With these synthetic inputs the plants in the soil get lazy, and the residues actually suppress the biological activity. Check it out."

Alison took his spade and dug a sample. "I can see it for myself. The topsoil's shallow. This earth feels pretty dead. There's not much humus, hardly any worms or insects."

Peter nodded. "After years of importing dirty energy, this is what you get: the ground's polluted, the fertility's rock bottom and you're into diminishing returns."

"I don't understand the last bit."

"Every year, the fertility in the soil gets less, and the residues increase. So the bang for the buck from your artificial fertilizer goes down: you put ever more fertilizer on the field each year to keep forcing the yield."

"So it's like a vicious circle," Alison said. "Where does it end?"

Peter shrugged. "What you're seeing here is so-called normal farming. Sometimes it really crashes. Maybe you get a resistant pest or weed that wipes the whole crop out. Or the water board jumps on you because of nitrate pollution. Sometimes it just keeps getting subtly worse."

Conversations like this are typical of the way I developed The Natural Advantage model. After the visit to Rookery Farm, I spent time with Alison looking at the energy sources she currently used in her work and the potential alternatives. We could both see that she faced the same problem as an intensive farm: growing dependence on forced energy inputs, declining productivity and quality, and a rising need for artificial additives to suppress the problems. As Alison put it, "I'm seeing my craving for red wine, cigarettes, and tranquillizers in a different light. My energy system is unsustainable."

Forced energy systems

There are some common aspects to the energy systems in conventional and organic farming: for example, sun and rain are clearly essential to both. However, the key source of energy and fertility is different. In conventional farming it is artificial fertilizer. This approach does not stimulate the natural cycle of growth, it short-circuits and inhibits it. Applying a narrow range of nutrients at the surface means that plants do not root deeply, nor do they draw in a wider range of other minerals from the soil. Chemical analysis shows that conventional crops have less iron, calcium, protein, and vitamin C compared to organic.

What energizes you in your work? Does your output well up naturally from within you, like plants growing from fertile ground? Or is your production driven by synthetic pressures? In many of the people and organizations I see, output is largely forced.

An easy test of this is whether your main motivators will lead to renewal, or to depletion and pollution. Here are some of the equivalents to artificial fertilizers I see in the typical work situation:

❖ Fear of losing face, losing your job, or simply losing control.
❖ Systematic pressure through performance culture, controls, targets, deadlines, aggressive bonus schemes.
❖ Competing for power or prestige.
❖ Pressure from managers, supervisors, or shareholders.

Natural energy

The main energy sources for organic farming are natural, plentiful, and free: sun, air, water, waste, and the biological activity in the earth. For many of these forces, the supply can't be controlled but it can be shaped, and an organic farmer ensures that these resources are harnessed. This is more a matter of stimulating and shaping natural processes than forcing, and it starts with cultivating ground condition.

The plant waste and animal manure on organic farms is a major energy source: recycling this as compost provides natural fuel for the earth and avoids the cost and problems of importing artificial fertilizer. Growing crops that renew the energy resources in the soil is another part of the organic way.

Human Energy Elements

In farming we are dealing essentially with physical energy flows. For example, an organic farmer can calculate a fertility budget estimating the inputs and outflows of key nutrients like nitrogen, to check if the overall energy cycle is sustainable. With people at work it's more subtle: we need to consider both tangible and intangible energy, and the interplay between them. If you are feeling emotionally stressed, this adds to the demand on your physical energy resources. Conversely, if you feel appreciated, this can enhance your physical energy, much like raising the biological activity in the soil.

The four types of human energy we will consider in this section are as interdependent and synergistic as the four elements in ground condition and plant growth.

Physical energy: the earth element

The biological activity in the earth is a kind of natural power station. It draws energy from air, water, sun, waste, and minerals. These are converted into fertility—energy in a form usable for plant growth. The earth is the growth medium in which the inputs combine, and healthy ground condition requires all four energy elements.

For human ground condition the type and quality of our physical inputs, especially food and drink, are a vital influence on our physical energy level. If we rely heavily on kick-start inputs, such as sugary foods and caffeinated drinks, this will create the same problem as artificial fertilizer in the earth; the price of the short-term boost is progressive clogging of our ability to renew vitality.

There are many other ways to cultivate physical energy besides good choice of diet. Aerobic exercise, which gets the circulation moving, has a significant benefit, as does relaxation. Most of us carry a good deal of stress in our body, which impairs physical vitality if it is not released. Even body posture can be important: good posture can improve our physical energy level, just as good soil structure helps fertility. Everything you do to improve the other three energies will help your physical condition too. If you feel positive, think clearly, and have a strong sense of purpose and vision, imagine how this can enhance your physical energy—and imagine how the opposite would reduce it.

The earth is also the source of a wide range of minerals required as nutrients for plant growth. Particular crops need specific nutrients: cabbage and green vegetables especially need calcium; sugar beet requires phosphorus. Healthy soil delivers a variety of nutrients better than do synthetic inputs and depleted soil. The parallel for human health is the minerals and vitamins we need in order to function effectively. Stress reduces our reserves of these. And the level of pollutants most of us have to deal with in our air, food, and water also puts heavy demands on these reserves. As a result, mineral and vitamin supplements are probably advisable to sustain physical ground condition.

In cultivating your physical energy, it's important to be observant and responsive. Many people respond to their physical ailments the way an intensive farmer treats weeds, simply grabbing a means to suppress the symptom. An organic farmer knows that a specific weed has a specific message: it is saying something about the condition of the soil and the response it requires. In the same way, if you know how to observe your physical condition, you can learn what you need to maintain your energy.

If you are willing to observe and respond to minor ailments, you may avoid some major ones. For example, when working under pressure from a deadline to complete part of this book, I developed mouth ulcers. This not only told me in broad terms that I was working unsustainably, it also had specific messages about my energy flows. On the physical level, it showed me that I needed more rest and more vitamin B. It also highlighted an emotional energy issue for me, a reluctance to receive nourishment and new ideas. Just as ground condition on the farm shows the state of all four elements, so our physical body will reflect issues from all four types of human energy. If you are mentally stagnant or emotionally unsettled, this affects your physical energy, and your body can highlight the issue for you if you observe it closely. This is a big subject in its own right: a good doorway to it is a personal development book called *You Can Heal Your Life* by Louise Hay.

Emotional energy: the water element

In relation to the growth of the plant and the life in the soil, water has two essential functions. First, it is a transmitter of energy and nutrients: it carries them down into the earth and up through the plant. Secondly, the hydrogen and oxygen in water are an energy source in their own right. However, water can also carry problems, such as diseases, or excess nitrates from artificial fertilizer. The system can be parched or swamped: too little or too much water both cause problems.

These properties of water provide pointers for emotional energy in human systems. The root meaning of emotion is outward movement. Our feelings are a significant means of transmitting energy and nutrition, both within the individual and between people. If I have a sense of purpose about a project, I can communicate it to myself and others with feeling, with love and appreciation. This positive emotional energy will nourish work output, just like watering a plant. I could also express this vision to myself with anger and self-criticism: "It's about time you put your back into something, you lazy time-waster." This would be like water carrying the kick-start of artificial fertilizer through the plant: it might prod me into action, but unsustainably.

Feelings can also operate in any of these ways in our interaction with others. At Alibi the productivity of the whole organization was limited by its dry ground condition, a culture focused on mental energy, where feelings were not expressed. The first step in addressing this was to develop the senior team's ability to handle emotions. We trained them in ways to let feeling flow through their work, without swamping it. As a result, productivity rose, nutrients could move through the system, and people could interact more easily with each other.

Water is a power source in its own right, and so are emotions. For example, appreciation is one of the best natural energizers. Remember a time when you felt deeply appreciated for a piece of work. Could you sense the flow of energy this created? Appreciation is a good example of clean energy: renewable and non-polluting. In contrast, strong negative emotions such as fear and anger can be seen as waste. They have high energy content, but need to be recycled to make them useful.

If you feel that your way of working or the culture in your organization is too dry, what can you do about it? It is quite easy to foster a climate of appreciation at work. The key is to develop the habit of appreciating more than you criticize. Appreciate yourself and others. This is likely to start a virtuous circle, a progressive spiral in which the working culture becomes more positive, more flowing, more fertile. In *Emotional Intelligence* Daniel Goleman discusses a number of research studies on how people learn best: it is by feeling recognized and appreciated for what they are doing right, however limited this may be, not by being criticized for what they've done wrong.

One of the barriers to positive emotional energy is that many people find it difficult to give or receive praise. A common reason for fearing praise is the expectation that it will be followed by criticism or a request for something. If you can start to change the expectation, you should start to change the experience too.

Water tends to spread, to permeate. In some situations this is a useful quality, but it can also cause problems. In everyday life, it is essential to channel water through plumbing and drainage systems. The same is true of emotional energy. We can easily be swamped or flooded by feelings if we cannot manage them. We may require a better drainage system: in human terms, this equates to methods for managing emotions, such as assertiveness and conflict resolution (see References). We may also require a better balance between the elements. If a piece of ground is waterlogged, air and warmth will help to dry it out. The analogy in your work is to engage your sense of purpose and perspective and your mental skills to help you clear an excess of emotion.

Mental energy: the fire element

In this model, fire or sun equates to mental energy. We often take too narrow a view of the mind's potential. Mental energy in the full sense includes not only logic and analysis, but also intuition and imagination, and the ability to combine them all. The sun's energy animates the life in the soil and the growth of the plant. In the same way, it is mental energy that enlivens our ground condition and fuels our output. Mental energy turns an idea into action, an inspiration into a tangible product.

Does this mean that all we have to do to fulfill a vision is to think about it? No. Mental energy in the full sense is fiery— there's more to it than thinking. It includes the heat of our will, our intent. It includes the bright light of insight, understanding, the flash of intuition, and the creative spark that ignites a process. It also includes the power of fire to consume and transform. To be productive, fire needs air, physical fuel, and something to heat; often water. If we can integrate our mental and emotional energy, the result is powerful, like steam.

If you look at the images you associate with fire, they should give you guidelines for generating and managing mental energy. The image I find helpful is to imagine my brain as a wood-burning stove. If the fuel is too wet, it's hard to start the fire, and I get choking smoke instead of useful heat. Conversely, if the fuel is too dry, I get high heat for a while but no sustained output. This metaphor highlights the subtle interplay between mental, emotional, and physical energy. We often think of emotion as impeding our brain, which it does at the extremes. However, the most productive mix, for plant and human growth, is moderate amounts of both heat and water. Used well, emotional energy can enrich our mental processes and our overall productivity.

Fire also needs air for combustion. To get the fire started and burning strongly, I need to open the stove's dampers wide and provide plenty of air. And to kill the flame, all I have to do is shut off the air flow. For me, this is a clear model of the connection between mental and inspirational energy. When I want to animate a new project, I need a strong sense of purpose and vision, and I need to convey this to my team to get their fire started. The vision needs to blow through and fuel the mental process, or you don't get productive heat.

Like fire, mental energy needs to be contained and directed to be of most use; without this, it can be highly destructive. This means regulating and balancing the supply of all four elements so that you get the amount of firepower you need for the job in hand. It also means developing a range of mental tools, such as analytical and intuitive methods, and ways to combine them. You can explore this further through the books mentioned in References.

In this book you have already seen examples of the two extremes of mental fire. Alison Martin was so swamped by negative feeling that her mental fire was out: she was unable to use her intelligence to dig herself out of work and personal stress. Stephen Lessing represents the other extreme. By over-using his mental powers, his whole ground condition became burned up and dried out. He drove himself to a state where his physical resources were exhausted and there was little air or water left in the soil. He had lost his sense of purpose and his capacity for feeling. In this state, more fire, mental effort, will only aggravate the problem. It takes rest, careful cultivation, and an inflow of air and water before the fire can be rekindled productively.

Inspirational energy: the air element

In organic growth, air has two essential functions. It is an enabler. Healthy soil has around 25 percent air content, and these spaces enable water, warmth, and air to circulate and interact with the earth to generate growth. Secondly, air is a source of fertility. It's understandable but ironic that humans often equate air with oxygen. In fact, 78 percent of our atmosphere is

nitrogen; in organic farming, air is a major source of this nutrient to fuel production.

The air element equates to inspirational energy, a sense of
higher purpose, wider perspective, and vision. The term inspiration, like the word spirit, derives from the Latin *spiritus,* meaning breath, air, or soul. What the organic model highlights is
how inspiration is needed to enable our fertility and productivity. It also shows us that vision and purpose are a powerful
energy source, a fuel for growth in their own right. Think about
outstanding achievement in any field: business, sport, the arts,
or your own work. Inspiration is part of the power we need for
peak performance.

Consider the qualities of air and how these also describe
inspirational energy. It is invisible, intangible, yet always around
us, available. If we are tense or defensive, our breath is usually
shallow and we don't access its full potential. As with water and
fire, both intent and technique can help us harness the power of
air more fully. In my own energy management, I find the link
between inspiration and breath very helpful. When I notice
myself tensing up, taking several long, slow breaths has many
benefits. It immediately gives me a sense of expansion and
relaxation, helping me to see the situation in better perspective
and to connect with my intention and purpose. Breathing more
deeply adds oxygen to the bloodstream, which enhances brain
activity, mental energy on which I can draw. It also helps to
release any physical and emotional stress I am feeling.

Accessing your inspirational energy can be as easy as breathing, but technique and process are also important. It is good to
find a visioning process which works for you, which enables
you to find clarity and purpose even in complex and confusing
situations. You may need to cultivate your ground condition
and soil structure to be able to harness the air element. For
example, compacted soil has little air circulation: this usually

equates to physical tension and depletion, which may need a concerted program to resolve. Relaxation, massage, yoga, or tai chi could all be helpful. Waterlogged soil also has poor air circulation and this is like being swamped by emotion; professional counseling could assist in clearing the situation. You will find examples of harnessing inspirational energy in the Caradon story later in this chapter, and in Financial Friends in Chapter 5.

Natural energy productivity

From the mechanistic viewpoint, energy is simply an input to achieve a desired output. A sack of fertilizer pushes out the crop. A gallon of gasoline gets you to the shopping mall. Setting a deadline and pressuring your subordinate produces the report you need. From the natural systems viewpoint, it is clear that energy doesn't disappear: it simply changes form. When energy is used in a process, the residual energy tends to disperse: this explains why the polluting residues of fossil fuels are so hard to clean up.

The organic farming model shows that if you harness natural energy in natural processes, the output and residues can also be clean and non-polluting. The "waste" residues can move on through the cycle, and natural processes can renew the value, the utility, of these dispersed forms of energy. Examples of this are biological activity in the soil, and the ability of plants to turn carbon dioxide into oxygen and carbon. It is important to see energy flows as a cycle, not as a linear flow. This is the start of raising energy productivity.

In a natural system, most of the energy need is met from recycling and from abundant sources. In a conventional, mechanistic, linear system, most of the energy inputs have to be expensively fabricated and tailored to the purpose. The difference is summed up in Figures 5 and 6.

It is useful to explore the parallel between plant growth and human productivity at work. The inputs to the plant include

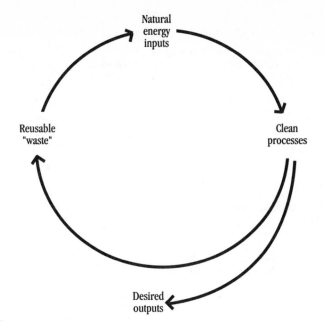

Figure 5 Natural energy cycle

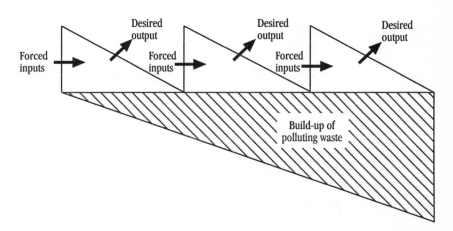

Figure 6 Linear energy process

clean, renewable energy such as sunlight, and "waste" such as carbon dioxide and waste matter in the soil. The processes by which the plant grows are clean, efficient, and non-polluting. The outputs of the plant's growth typically include a useful crop, such as tomatoes or wheat grain, desirable by-products

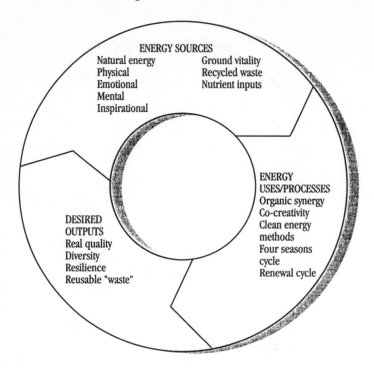

ENERGY SOURCES
Natural energy   Ground vitality
Physical   Recycled waste
Emotional   Nutrient inputs
Mental
Inspirational

**ENERGY
USES/PROCESSES**
Organic synergy
Co-creativity
Clean energy
methods
Four seasons
cycle
Renewal cycle

**DESIRED
OUTPUTS**
Real quality
Diversity
Resilience
Reusable "waste"

Figure 7 Personal energy cycle

such as oxygen, and "waste" that is biodegradable and reusable. If we map these stages on to human work, the cycle could look as in Figure 7.

Personal Energy Management in Practice

Learning to apply clean energy principles in your work is like learning a new sport. It takes time and practice to get your eye in, to learn what to look for, and to develop your range of responses. Don't fade if your early moves feel like three steps forward and two back. You probably have a range of habits and dependencies to change.

Asking yourself "How's my energy?" may be too loose to be useful. Checking your ground condition, including the four energy elements, can be a quick and practical approach. Using the tangible analogy of earth—physical, water—emotional, fire—mental, and air—inspirational should help you with action as well as understanding; following through on the analogy can give you specific pointers on how to manage your energy use. You will find additional methods for personal energy management in later chapters. For example, recycling waste energy is covered in Chapter 5; mental and inspirational energy methods in Chapter 6. *The Work Easy Workbook*, listed under References, is a self-help book devoted to this subject.

The Personal Energy Audit

This audit is designed to give you an overview of your main energy inflows and outflows, so that you can set yourself priorities for managing your energy better and identify issues requiring investigation.

The audit is not intended to be exhaustive, and is not a substitute for professional help where needed, for example a comprehensive medical health check, advice on diet and exercise tailored to your needs, or counseling regarding major emotional issues.

Use the checklist overleaf to assess the main energy inflows and outflows in your working life. The processes in which you use energy should be considered as outflows. The specific items listed are not meant to be comprehensive; space is provided for you to add other items that are significant to you. For each one, rate its importance on a scale of 0 (unimportant) to 10 (highly important). As you go through, put an asterisk in the Review Priority column for items you feel need urgent consideration. Remember that some items may be both a source and a use of energy.

Initially, do these ratings for your current way of working; you may wish to do the exercise again, to see how much impact a different approach would have. Also, remember that outflows include those that are desirable and productive, and those that dissipate or misuse energy.

	Energy Inflow	Energy Outflow	Review Priority
PHYSICAL			
The activities of your work itself			
Other activity related to your work, e.g. commuting, preparing for work, winding down afterwards			
Diet: "healthy," sustaining food/drink			
"unhealthy" food/drink			
Breathing			
Exercise			
Relaxation			
Other			
....			
....			
....			

	Energy Inflow	Energy Outflow	Review Priority
EMOTIONAL			
Self-appreciation or put-down: supporting or blaming yourself, e.g. when results are not "successful"			
Appreciation or negativity from your boss			
Appreciation or negativity from colleagues at work			
Feelings expressed toward you by people you work with (including colleagues, customers)			
The general attitude to feelings where you work: can feelings be voiced, or are they suppressed?			
The emotional rewards or pressures of your job content			
The emotional rewards or pressures of the whole organization			
How do you respond to unexpected changes at work? Are they typically a stimulus or a stress for you?			
Support/antagonism from family and friends			
The emotional rewards or demands of your leisure time/hobbies			
Other:			
....			
....			
....			

	Energy Inflow	Energy Outflow	Review Priority

MENTAL

Does the content of your work, and the way you choose to do it, give you mental stimulus or exhaustion?

Does the organization you work in give you mental stimulus or exhaustion?

Is your habitual way of thinking positive and creative, or do you tend to worry and fret and focus on the negatives?

Do you use both logical and intuitive skills in your work, and integrate them?

Do uncertainty and conflicting data stimulate or dissipate your mental energy?

Do you have activities outside work (e.g. family, friends, hobbies) that give you mental stimulus or exhaustion?

Other ....

....

....

....

	Energy Inflow	Energy Outflow	Review Priority

INSPIRATIONAL

Do you have a sense of purpose and inspiration in your work?

Does the organization you work for have a true sense of purpose and service that helps to inspire your work?

Do you have a mentor, boss, or colleague at work who is a role model for you in bringing spiritual energy to work?

When your work gets demanding or exhausting, can you re-energize yourself by remembering the point of it all?

Do you have a sense of purpose and inspiration in your life generally?

In your free time, do you choose any activities that inspire you (e.g. through nature, music, meditation, or do you choose distractions or compensations for stress and fatigue?

Other: ....

....

....

....

Review

When you have finished the audit, add your inflow and outflow scores for each of the four energy types and then total them. If you are running an energy surplus, congratulations! If you are running an energy deficit in your work, ask yourself what is causing this. Are you drawing energy from the rest of your life to fund the deficit in your work, or are you exhausting your energy reserves?

As you review your audit, look particularly at items you have asterisked for further attention. Chose up to five of these as specific priorities for immediate action. Consider how you would like your energy habits to change in these areas, how you can get more advice or information, and how you might set about making a change.

When you start to convert to sustainable methods of work, I recommend that you use the Personal Energy Audit as a way of measuring your progress and steering your priorities. It can also help you evaluate major decisions about your job or lifestyle in advance.

Natural Energy in Organizations

The principle of using natural energy to achieve sustained production applies to organizations as well as to individuals. However, applying the organic way is more difficult once we move beyond the individual. Any organization develops norms, culture, and operating methods that tend to institutionalize a mechanistic approach.

Although command-and-control hierarchies are unfashionable, newer approaches are also often unsustainable. Empowerment and self-direction can leave teams and individuals under even more stress than before, because there are insufficient skills and support. The pressure for performance keeps growing, and there may be less scope to define expectations and negotiate an acceptable workload. On the other hand, dispersed power structures create more scope for groups or individuals to reshape their way of working.

In moving an organization to natural energy methods, delivering results remains a paramount concern. Unless top management and stakeholders are exceptionally understanding, predictable outcomes are still required. The challenge is to achieve them through organic methods that are inherently less controllable.

There are many ways to make this difficult transition possible. It can be done by evolution, not revolution: developing the skills first, trialing new approaches, operating on "dual voltage." The key deliverables can be used as a touchstone, a sanity test of each new move. It also helps to form a vision of *improving* results through natural energy methods, not just maintaining them. It should be possible over time to achieve higher output, more value, better quality, and closer customer dialogue.

Most organizations have two main energy problems. They are dependent on forced-energy inputs, and they have an imbalance between the four energy elements. They are preoccupied with mental and physical energy, with thinking and doing. In terms of the four elements, there is too much earth and fire and not enough water and air. As a result the culture, the ground condition, is hard, hot, dry, and compacted. There is little space for the flow of feelings, or for the energy arising from genuine vision and inspiration.

The way to correct this energy imbalance is through a mix of intent and technique. If top management or team leaders can change their habits, this will permeate to others. When people can express and receive feelings, both positive and negative, the ground condition of the organization becomes more fertile and receptive.

Many organizations produce vision, purpose, or value statements. Sadly, many of these are just another synthetic, external input, and are regarded skeptically by most people both within and outside the organization. Often such statements are developed by a handful of people, acting unilaterally and in isolation. For a vision to energize an organization, there needs to be scope for people at all levels to contribute, to feel part of a creative dialogue. And too many vision statements grow from mental energy, not from the heart and soul, not from the emotional and truly inspirational levels. The question of how to create and work with a sustainable vision is explored further in Chapter 6.

Caradon

In early 1985, I was managing director of Redland Lumex, a relatively small, misfit business that Redland had decided to divest. I was ready for a new adventure, and unknown to me it was on the way. My boss, Peter Jansen, had a superb eye for acquisitions. He had realized years before that Reed, the large publishing group, would eventually simplify its portfolio and sell off its building products business. He patiently cultivated contacts within Reed, and when the company reached this decision in 1985, Redland was offered first refusal on Reed Building Products. At that point, Peter asked me to look at RBP with him. We were excited by the prospect. Both of us had started in consumer marketing, and were attracted by the potential of some of the best brands in UK building materials such as Twyfords and Mira. In ground condition terms, RBP was fertile but sleepy soil. We felt inspired and enthused: we could see what the business needed and we had the vision and skills to achieve it.

Redland turned down our strong recommendation to buy Reed Building Products. The group chief executive, Colin

Corness, was wary of consumer marketing. He said he would rather expand into quarries in Texas than brand names in Britain. This left me deeply uncertain about my own future. I had joined Redland in 1983 intending to build my career with the company, and RBP would have been the perfect move.

I returned from a subsequent holiday to receive a phone call at home from Peter Jansen. "Alan, something interesting has come up. Could you drop over to my house to talk about it?" It was rare for Peter to call me at home, and I sensed that he could hardly contain his excitement; I went straight over. Peter explained that he was considering leading a management buy-in of Reed Building Products. Candover, one of the leading London venture capitalists, was seriously interested in backing it. Would I like to join him as his number two: as an executive director of the group, a founding investor, and as managing director of Twyfords Bathrooms? I can still recall the feeling at that moment. It was like standing in front of an open goal in a soccer Cup Final, with the ball at your feet. I felt completely clear about saying yes to the proposal.

We started Caradon with £7 million of share capital, and £53 million of borrowings. In the previous 12 months, Reed Building Products had sales of £119 million, and pretax profit of £7 million. Two years later, after some divestments, sales were £142 million, profit was £16 million. In summer 1985, less than two years after its founding, Caradon floated on the London Stock Exchange. The share offer was 40 times oversubscribed; the group's market valuation was £134 million, and it rose rapidly thereafter. How did we achieve this?

The power of clean energy

Peter Jansen and I both had a highly intuitive approach to our work. This grew from principles that were largely unarticulated and neither of us was much into formal values statements. Our approach can readily be understood in terms of clean energy principles and the four elements.

Air

The business inspired us, and we inspired it. We felt a passion for the people, the products, brand names, factories, and the customers they served. We had a vigorous, clear sense of vision, seeing the fuller potential in this situation.

People are often demoralized when the business they work for is sold. The reverse was true with Caradon. As many people explained to us, they had for several years sensed that Reed International had no vision or purpose for RBP. Now they knew that their leaders had put their houses on the line to buy into the business. The Caradon era was welcomed as a breath of fresh air.

Bringing air into the organization involved opening it up, creating a more free-flowing culture, with direct personal contact. The RBP style had been impersonal and hierarchical, with a preference for written reports. In the early years the Caradon head office had three key people: Peter Jansen, Danny Cohen our finance director, and myself. We moved around the organization a lot, extending our roots into it and opening up the soil structure in the process. We made a point of expressing our enthusiasm about the people and the business, and gradually our inspiration permeated to them. Being shareholders as well as directors, we could link the vision and purpose of the organization as a whole to the operating companies and their particular issues.

Water

The culture we inherited from RBP was dry. The language its head office in central London spoke to the operating companies was mostly financial and technical. In contrast, we expressed our feelings and asked others to tell us theirs. There were stacks of issues and inefficiencies to address, but we were working with good-hearted people.

Intriguingly, Caradon's massive borrowings created camaraderie. No one reproached the new leadership for it: they understood that we had taken a carefully judged business risk and backed it with our personal financial commitment. There was some fear and insecurity about whether we'd succeed and what changes would be needed. But the fear led to action, not rumors and inertia. We encouraged people to voice their fears and anxieties: they learned that these would be heard and considered, with no attempt to reproach or suppress them. By hearing and exploring the negatives, it was possible to clarify and recycle the energy they contained.

One of the qualities of the early Caradon years was flow: a relatively easy forward flow in business initiatives, decisions, communication. I attribute this largely to the way we brought the feeling element into the culture, so that this energy was available positively to all of us. Even the need to make several hundred people redundant early on did not knock the appreciation culture. We spoke face to face with the people who were leaving, valuing what they had contributed and admitting our own sadness at having to make such cuts. The response from almost all the leavers was support and understanding for our approach.

Fire

The amount and quality of mental energy that Caradon applied to turning its businesses around was outstanding. Peter, Danny, and myself all had different styles. Mine was more like the fire of a blowtorch, probing into blockages, heating up the facts of a situation to expand and reshape it. Peter's fire was more like lamplight, gentle but penetrating. His style was to ask a few questions, but the right ones, and to keep them burning steadily until they were answered. Danny was like an inviting fire in a cottage hearth. He had a conversational style to which people warmed. They would open up naturally to him, and his gentle questioning would elicit crucial information very effectively. People knew that both Peter and Danny had an iron fist inside the glove: if the easy style didn't work, they would be firm in confronting the issue.

All three of us were keen to stimulate and harness the knowledge and intelligence of the whole organization. We did this with our direct subordinates and encouraged them to do the same. We also conversed with people at every level. As the soil structure and the culture opened up, so air could circulate and the fire burn brighter. The business turnaround was good not only because of strategic thinking at the top, but also because we harnessed mental energy at every level and enabled a mass of operational improvements. This happened through culture and example, and through project teams, consultants, and suggestion schemes—real ones with genuine recognition and rewards.

Earth

When Caradon began it had high potential fertility. People were more dormant than depleted. Along with air, water, and heat, what this soil needed was more biological activity so that the whole organizational organism became more dynamic. We stimulated this in many ways. Exploring previously ignored problems and tapping unused intelligence throughout the organization was like activating and recycling an immense pile of waste.

We created a high degree of movement, new connections with often no immediate performance goal, but which paid off handsomely by stimulating ground condition. For example, Peter, a golf lover, introduced a Caradon Golf Day, which brought together people from all levels and parts of the organization. At Twyfords, I organized visits to the factories for our employees' families and for our customers. Such initiatives created a groundswell more valuable than any amount of top-down directives. The whole organization became enthusiastic, with many individuals and teams improving the infrastructure of the business, much as biological activity conditions the soil.

5
Composting Waste

Every output becomes a useful input: this is one of the basic principles of an organic system. However, this is not recycling as we have come to think of it. What image does the word bring up for you? Perhaps collection bins for paper, glass, or cans. All good stuff, but these are mechanical systems. You get less out than you put in, and it takes substantial energy to achieve even this.

The difference in a natural system is that recycling can be synergistic: you get out *more* usable energy than you put in, and the energy achieving this is mostly clean and costless. To emphasize the difference from mechanical recycling I have used the term composting.

Composting is by far the most important of the ways an organic farmer recycles waste. It involves transforming animal and plant waste into a major energy source for future growth. In essence, composting is a biological process that can be initiated and shaped by human intervention. Using it requires care in collection, handling, and application, but the principles and methods employed in organic farming show how we can harness the fertility of our waste issues at work. As you adopt the principles of ground condition and natural energy in your work, you will develop the capacity to compost human energy waste as a major source of fertility.

This chapter considers four types of human energy waste, aligning with the four elements: physical, emotional, mental, and inspirational. In this context, we can define waste as energy whose form impairs our productivity and sustainability. The waste we are considering here is primarily intangible, although negative energy such as anger or anxiety often creates physical stress.

Choosing to Get Angry

My personal development is my research and development lab. It's my chance to explore way-out ideas, some of which I refine for the business world. In April 1999, I spent two weeks in Hawaii, learning from a Kahuna. This is the name given to teachers of the Hawaiian native tradition, a set of principles evolved through generations of tribal culture, living closely with the land and ocean. In my first few days with Kahu, I was forced to realize that my outlook was more narrow and western than I had thought.

"Alan, you keep asking how to," Kahu said. "You're looking for techniques again, trying to box me up and pin me down. You should be looking for the goddamn principles." He slammed his fist on the wall—as often, moving from gentle to fierce without pause. Slowly I learned to listen, fully listen, instead of seeking the next cue for a clever question. I realized that whether Kahu was talking about cooking fish, making love, or designing buildings, the principles were visible and they were common to everything.

Each morning we were asked to spend several hours performing strenuous, repetitive physical exercises. I longed for a crisp kickoff presentation with overheads, to summarize the objectives. All we were told was that this was preparation. After a couple of days I told Kahu, "I can't go on with this. My whole body is aching. I'm exhausted."

Kahu looked keenly at me. "Do you know what I do when I'm tired and flat?" I shook my head. "I get myself angry."

I was stunned. "You mean, you deliberately make yourself angry?"

Kahu flashed me a roguish grin. "Sure. If I've got a big session and I'm down, it's the fastest way to get some energy. Try it. Try getting mad about how pointless these dumb exercises are, and see if it gets you moving." He went off laughing to have a coffee break, leaving the group to repeat the same movement for another hour or two.

The main principle behind the exercises Kahu gave us was to keep moving. "Whatever comes up, whatever you feel, bring it into the movement, don't stop." Now that I let myself, I got really furious about these exercises, being left in a room to do them for hours with no explanation. The effect of this anger on my body was powerful and actually delightful. Instead of dragging myself through the movements slowly, with aching limbs, my whole body was energized. The movements became easy, and by lunchtime I felt refreshed, not depleted. I thought how differently I'd have handled this in a typical British workshop. I would have sneaked out of the group and gone for a tea break, with my negative feelings festering, suppressed.

Back in the UK a few weeks later, I had the chance to apply Kahu's teachings in earnest. I was immersed in writing this book and I felt completely stuck. The writing was going slowly and lacked sparkle. The publisher was niggling, and I felt tired, dejected. Then I remembered a scene from my favorite Marx

Brothers movie, *Duck Soup*. Groucho Marx as Rufus Firefly, President of the tinpot Republic of Fredonia, winds himself into a fury over a trifling insult.

I strode up and down the room, ranting grandly, trusting that my secretary next door would understand as usual. "This is pathetic," I told myself loudly. "A man of all my talents floundering around like this! Eight pages in two days! It's appalling: I can do better than this. Just watch me!" If a waterlogged field gets air and warmth, it becomes highly fertile very quickly. In the same way, by applying purpose and mental energy to my dejection, I got myself moving productively. My feelings of discouragement were useless waste, but there was plenty of power in them to be used.

Human Energy Waste

Every organization tells us that people are its most valuable resource. So it makes sense that the most valuable, fertile waste arises from the people: human energy waste. People take in and use a lot of energy in their work, and inevitably some of this becomes waste. After all, none of us is 100 percent efficient!

The compost cycle on organic farms provides a superb blueprint for recycling human energy waste in the workplace. On the farm, this is a physical process that needs to run its course over several months. With human energy waste, the process can take anywhere from seconds to years. It can be applied to minor operational issues, or to such fundamentals as the purpose of your work. In the work context, composting is a process that individuals and teams can learn to apply for themselves. However, it is a powerful transformational process requiring experience and specific skills. It may be wise to get professional help to help you recycle the most difficult waste: emotional and spiritual issues, and interpersonal conflicts. I offer you direct guidelines for going through the process yourself, but use discretion about when to do so unaided.

The alchemy of compost

The ancient alchemists sought to turn base matter into gold. Composting achieves this. It starts with rubbish, animal excrement, rotting vegetable matter, straw, even weeds. All this "waste," useless in these forms, ends up as humus, highly fertile, rich in biological activity, able to renew the earth's vitality.

There are several methods of composting: some depend on the use of air, i.e. they are "aerobic;" some depend on excluding it, i.e. they are "anaerobic." The temperature in the process may be cool, warm, or hot. I have chosen to talk here about hot aerobic composting, a common method in Britain, because it offers the best parallel for the human system.

Although some farm waste can be reused without composting it, the composting process has many benefits. It creates more fertility and can recycle complex waste. The high temperature in hot composting kills weed seeds; it breaks complex proteins into simpler, more usable compounds; it generates antibiotics and pest resistance; it produces extra nitrogen and fixes it in bacterial form, accessible by the plants. An American study found that one-quarter of the quantity of compost relative to ordinary manure was required to produce the same yield benefits. Composting has many hallmarks of a natural process. It is complex in detail, but simple in concept; it is powerful and clean; and it is synergistic—you get more out than you put in.

Seven Tips for Good Compost

This summary of the main principles of hot aerobic composting on the farm gives an indication of how they apply to human energy waste.

Collection

To get the benefit of the composting process, waste materials have to be gathered and brought together. This is a significant investment of labor, and when you're dealing with animal excrement it may not be very pleasant! In the same way, your first step is to identify and gather the waste in your work. This requires patience, good observation, and resilience. Your waste may include difficult feelings and project failures that have a pungent smell and that you might rather bury.

Finding your rubbish takes both peripheral and focused vision. You need to see where it has been buried and suppressed or thrown out to the edges of your ecosystem, the equivalent of waste ground where trash gets dumped. Start with physical waste, reviewing tensions and ailments using the approach described on page 56. Then consider mental waste: contradictions, unresolved questions. Why did that project fail? Why did that customer really switch their account? Facing such questions reveals their emotional content: many issues that may seem entirely rational also involve our feelings. Observe your feelings as clearly as you can: this is all part of the collection stage.

Next, gather the emotional waste, identifying the tensions and where you feel stressed in your work. Go into this, identify the sources, such as particular responsibilities or relationships. Keep breathing as you do this, aerating the compost. Explore any negative feelings you have in your work, such as fear, anxiety, uncertainty, anger. Use as much mental clarity as you can to understand the causes of these feelings. Think of these waste feelings as a flow of energy that has been impeded and see what outcome would unblock them. What is it your energy wants to flow towards? Possibly you are angry because someone has not acknowledged you, or fearful because you haven't faced the implications of losing your job and the constructive alternatives this could open up.

Negative inspirational energy can be the most depleting and the most difficult to face. A sense of pointlessness about some or all of your work is like a major pollution problem: pervasive and hard to clear. Use the parallel with air pollution: it can arise from a single main source like a dirty factory, or from a diffuse problem like road traffic. Either way, a systemic change is probably needed: a switch to clean energy sources and processes, including recycling.

In counseling it is often said that expressing a problem is already half way to resolving it. Gathering and identifying your waste issues is a significant step in the recycling process. It helps to record and describe in detail the issues—both the facts and your feelings—don't just use shorthand labels. And avoid judging yourself or the issue as far as possible.

Heaping

The waste needs to be heaped up, so that there is a sufficient mass of material for the biological processes to start and sustain themselves. If the heap is too low, the process may not begin. If it is too high or dense, parts of the heap will lack air and the process will be incomplete.

Pile your problems on top of each other and heap the waste up. Spreading your negatives thinly or scattering them at the edges of your field will not recycle the thorny ones and won't give you the maximum juice. Adopt Peter Norman's approach of sending in the pigs: "Sometimes in farming, when you're in a bit of a mess, the best way through is to make a complete mess, churn it all up good and proper." You are initiating a process that may be scary, that is beyond your conscious control, but that can really move you forward.

You build your compost heap by facing your waste issues fully and deeply. Be prepared to face them all, whatever aspect of your work they relate to, whatever type of energy level they represent.

If this leaves you feeling overwhelmed or despairing, allow the feeling, observe it, and don't deny it or judge it. Keep your sense of purpose and perspective: remember that you are more than your feelings. Adapt the Buddhist mantra: "I feel fearful, but I am not my fear." And ensure that you have support available to you.

Air supply

A plentiful supply of air is essential to fuel the biological activity in the hot aerobic composting process. Hence the compost heap must be shaped so that air can be drawn in from the sides. If the air supply is inadequate, some or all of the heap will not reach peak temperature, desired breakdowns will not occur in the waste material, and weed seeds will not be killed.

At the most basic level, this means that when you feel strong emotions, keep breathing! It also means that you have to sustain your composting process by affirming your sense of purpose and perspective. Keep believing that there's gold in your muck, a positive reason for the upheavals. You need inspirational energy to fuel this transformation.

Water content

The ideal moisture content in a compost heap is quite high: 55–70 percent. As with ground condition, too much or too little will stifle activity. If the heap is waterlogged, air is excluded and it will not heat up.

Relating this to your work, if you are too dry, if you deny or repress your feelings, biological recycling is stifled. Exploring the issues with a friend or counselor may give you the encouragement and sense of safety to achieve this. Conversely, if you are swamped by your feelings and the compost heap is sodden, the waste will fester, not transform. In this situation, your compost needs more heat and air: mental clarity, constructive enquiry, and a sense of perspective.

Heat

High temperature is central to this process of transforming muck into gold. Micro-organisms combine with air and moisture to generate heat through decomposing the waste. As the temperature rises, the more complex material is broken down and becomes fuel to continue the process. At its peak, the heat may reach 70°C.

Relating this to the four human energy elements, it highlights the importance of our intelligence in composting our energy waste. The process should generate heat, mental energy, which can then take the process further. You should find that composting your waste issues generates fresh understanding, clear thinking to move you forward.

Turning

To get the full benefit of the process, it is common to turn the heap after a few weeks. Turning means inverting the compost to aerate it. This is done in the cooling-down phase and initiates a repeat of the cycle. Turning the compost heap increases the air supply and renews the recycling process. The effect is to achieve fuller breakdown of the waste and higher humus content.

My experience of human energy composting is that the process is largely self-directing and has its own momentum. It can be tiring and distressing, but I have learned to trust it. Periodically I am aware of this process going on within me and have to give it my attention, but I don't have to make it happen. In your own recycling scheme, review your progress occasionally, see where it is leading you, and bring the qualities of air, purpose, and perspective into it.

Application

The timing and method of application of compost are important to derive full benefit from it. The aim is to incorporate the compost into the soil as quickly and fully as possible; in this way the extra humus acts as a catalyst for the rest of the soil. The ideal season for application is autumn: the compost will stimulate further build-up of fertility ready for the demands of spring crops. Frequent spreading in thin layers is preferable to one heavy application.

The main moral of this for workplace waste is about timing. It is best to recycle your waste some time before you place a peak output demand on yourself. Allow time for absorption.

Befriending Your Weeds

An organic farm has many other useful waste flows besides the compost cycle. Waste residues are often recycled directly. When most crops are harvested, the roots are left in the ground and the nutrients in them return to the soil. While this is also true for conventional farms, the effect is greater in the organic system. The root systems are bigger and healthier, and the higher biological activity in organic soil means the waste is more fully broken down.

On a conventional farm, weeds would simply be seen as a problem: an undesirable waste product to be stamped out as fully as possible. For the organic farmer, weeds are a good example of the gift in the problem. I remember asking Peter Norman at Magdalen Farm how he dealt with weeds. He replied, "The first thing to understand is the message. When you get a particular species of weed in a particular place, it'll tell you something quite specific that you need to respond to. For example, if I see tansy or procumbent pearlwort, I know the soil's got severe compaction. If I see buttercups or coltsfoot, I know the drainage is poor. If I see nettles or docks, it tells me the nitrogen level is high."

The conventional farming approach to weeds treats them as an enemy to be eliminated. Herbicides are sold under such brand names as Commando, Avenger, and Crusader. The organic farmer treats weeds more like a dissident minority group: they may be antagonistic to the mainstream, but fruitful coexistence is possible. Weeds can actually assist the main crop. Sometimes they attract pests away from it; often they are home to predators that will consume the pests before the pests consume the main crop. Hence organic farmers will leave wide field margins for the weeds to grow, and may even include weed strips interspersed in a large field of cereal.

Can you see a parallel here for your work? Do you or your organization stamp out anything or anyone that diverges from the immediate output task? If you find a dissident voice in yourself or your team, I suggest you treat it as the organic farmer handles weeds. Learn from it, tolerate it, keep it within reasonable bounds, and see how to use it instead of eradicating it. The alternative is likely to be progressively declining fertility and rising ground pollution.

Financial Friends

Financial Friends was a small client for me, just a two-person partnership, but their problems looked so thorny that I was drawn by the challenge. Phil and Marion Wood had started this business while they were married and set it up as a formal partnership when they divorced, four years before I met them. Their business was financial advice, selling pension plans and life insurance to private individuals. Marion dealt with generating sales leads, handling enquiries, appointments, and paperwork. Phil met the clients and drafted the proposals.

"I never thought I'd say this, but I'm sick of this business." Phil was slumped behind his desk. "I've no appetite for it any more. It's depressing me, my whole life is affected by it."

Marion sat stiffly, her arms crossed, and looked at him

witheringly. "You always get so dramatic, you take it all personally. I wish you'd face the practicalities instead." She turned to
me. "The basic problem, Alan, is that the business is under-
performing. I think it's due to some kind of communication
problem between Phil and myself. That's what we want you to
fix."

I had a strong sense of two people hooked on their own,
irreconcilable scripts. In ground condition terms, Phil was
waterlogged, Marion was dry and hard as rock. It was a daunting task to engender openness and flow so that they could
explore the real issues and communicate with each other. I sug-
gested that the best next step was an individual session for me
with each of them, and they welcomed this idea with relief.

As I prepared for my session with Marion, I was unsure how
to reach her. Beneath her hard crust of logical criticism, I suspected she had buried a lot of feelings about the marriage and
the business partnership with Phil. I took my usual "park and
ride" approach: using my conscious mind to clarify the question, and then leaving my subconscious to come up with an
answer. That afternoon, driving through country lanes in sultry
June weather, I started to think about thunderstorms. When it
gets really hot for a while, summer storms blow up, and you get
torrential rain. I started laughing: I realized that this image gave
me an approach with Marion. I could see how a natural process
could be harnessed to help her open to the water element and
start moving the feelings that were clogging and polluting her
system.

Stoking up a storm

When we met, I was even more analytical than Marion. I plied
her with questions and we piled up a stack of observations on
the problems of the business. Most of them were due to Phil.
Although she stayed sharply logical, I could sense that Marion

was getting increasingly tense and heated as the issues were heaped together. I sought to step up the heat and to lead her toward expressing her feelings. Aiming to pile the waste higher, I voiced my own emotions about it strongly. At the same time, I made a link to the air element and the overall vision of the business. My guiding image was of the hot, sultry wind that often precedes a summer storm.

"Marion," I said, "I feel really upset by all these concerns you are listing. These are major problems, serious…"

"Very serious." Marion was twisting her hands as she spoke.

"I've got to tell you, I feel really worried for the future of the business. You and Phil have both put so much into this partnership, it's got so much potential, but it's obviously under serious threat."

"Very serious." Marion was staring into space.

"What also really upsets me, Marion, is how this affects you. Where does it leave you? I can't imagine how you're feeling…"

"Feeling!" The storm broke. She leapt to her feet, shouting, picked up the vase from her dining table and threw it so hard that it shattered on the wall. "Feeling! I want to kill him! How can I get it right with a man like that?"

For some time Marion stormed on, alternating between rage at Phil and weeping with a pent-up mixture of sadness, pain, and frustration. Remembering how the heat needs to rise in the early stage of composting, I urged her to let the feelings flow instead of trying to calm her down.

As Marion became quieter, I raised questions about purpose and perspective, to aerate and turn the compost. "Do you still have a sense of vision for Financial Friends?" I asked her. "How would you like to see the business develop from here?"

These questions certainly renewed the composting process. I was impressed that Marion was already combining feelings, thoughts, and perspective. "Alan, the point is, Financial Friends is Phil and me. You can't have a vision for this business without having a vision of how the two of us relate. That's what I feel desperate about."

"Desperate?"

"Well, desperate in my confusion. I have this sense that we have negative patterns between us, going back years, and it's exhausted us. But what I can't see at all is, could both of us change enough to make it work properly?"

Turning the compost

The ferment intensified again. I felt I was coaching an improvisational jazz quartet, using my questions to draw in whichever of the four elements seemed faintest.

Marion started pacing restlessly around the room. I took this as a good sign that her energy was getting moving. "It's always been like this with Phil. I try to do my part perfectly. Then if there's any problem, it must be his fault."

I nodded. "So how do you feel toward him now?"

She clenched her fists. "Angry! Oh yes, angry. Bloody furious, in fact."

I stood up and came closer to her. "So what I suggest is, intensify the feeling. Picture the scenes that upset you, remember how the business is suffering, and feel your fury. Speak to him. Do you want to pick an object to represent him?"

Marion smiled. "OK. The television set can be Phil. I'll get as good a hearing from the telly as I would from him."

She kept pacing the room, and I could see the tension rising in her body, until at last she started shouting. As the raw rage passed, the fertile insight that emerged was: "I can't achieve anything except through you, Phil."

At this point, I intervened. "So you're still furious, but now you can see why. Right?"

She nodded. "Right."

"Keep feeling the fury, and ask yourself a question. Forget Phil: What would you like to do with this anger? You've got this terrific energy you've unleashed: How do you want to use it? Imagine that you can achieve things without him. What do you want to achieve? Keep walking, keep feeling the anger, but breathe it, circulate it."

She looked puzzled. "What do you mean, circulate it?"

I came over and stood next to her. "Where in your body do you feel the anger?"

She held her stomach. "Here. Definitely."

"OK. So as you breathe, imagine breathing this anger up your spine, through your brain, down to your heart, and back to your stomach. Think of the anger like steam: it's scalding, but there's a power you can harness. Picture these questions like the pistons in a steam engine: you feed the anger in, and you can get forward motion out."

There was a long silence. Marion walked slowly around the room. I could actually watch the cycle of her breathing in, moving the energy up, confronting the question, and then releasing the energy to continue the cycle. After a while she sat down, eyes closed, still composting. Eventually she opened her eyes and smiled at me.

"This is such a relief," she said. "At least I've got past blaming someone else. I can see that I'm quite skilled and capable, and I have blind spots too. I'm not good at seeing clients, it's not my scene. But I don't have to depend on Phil for it." She smiled again, radiantly. "When I feel my power of choice, it gets quite clear. We could bring in a second sales consultant, and I can channel the leads through them. Or we could dissolve the partnership and I could use my skills elsewhere."

"And how do you feel about those options?"

"I'm happy with either of them. I just feel confident I won't have to live with the crap any more."

Draining the swamp

My initial session with Phil was quite different, but also fruitful. What he needed was air and drainage, not air and water. Feeling swamped by a sense of helplessness and hopelessness was a familiar and even comfortable place for him, his way of escaping blame. He was reluctant to open to a sense of purpose or perspective, which would aerate the compost heap.

I helped him to find it by asking him to remember the vision and excitement he felt at the start of the business. I also pressed him to face the implications of things going on as they were. We began to analyze his feelings and the repeating patterns between him and Marion. This helped to drain off some of his emotion and bring his mental energy to bear, raising heat to help the process.

When the three of us met again, the energy of the session was clean and vibrant. They both wanted to move forward: to agree an overall goal for the business and steps to achieve it. They could see that when Marion denied emotion and Phil drowned in it, the issues never got faced. "I'll tell you what, Marion," Phil said. "I'd like to agree a no-blame clause between us."

Marion smiled. "What do you mean?"

"Let's agree that neither of us will blame the other for the current situation. We are where we are. I want to decide where we go next, not whose fault it was in the first place."

My work with Financial Friends is on-going, although slowly. It is too soon to say if sustainable principles will take root in the business. There have been some lasting changes in Marion: she is more strong in herself, more independent, able to use and express her emotional energy. She has also found some independent channels for her abilities. Although Phil has responded positively in our sessions together, he has been reluctant to change his old habits. It is still easier for him to wallow in helplessness than come out and face the issues. The potential synergy of the partnership has not yet been achieved, but like many natural processes, change on this scale has its own pace and can't be forced.

Composting Waste in Organizations

In any energy process, the ideal is to use clean fuel and clean methods that achieve the result without pollution. The typical approaches in many organizations are far from this: they often rely on forced-energy inputs. These processes may seem logistically efficient, but they make poor use of human energy and generate waste problems that are rarely addressed. Here are a few examples of how energy waste can arise in working relationships:

❖ Backbiting between production and sales departments, blaming each other for delivery problems.
❖ Unresolved tensions between an old-school, highly analytical boss and an intuitive, creative subordinate.
❖ A project team making superhuman efforts preparing a bid for a major contract, but finding it awarded to a competitor.
❖ Two directors jockeying for position, competing for power, both wanting to succeed the current chief executive.
❖ A company hitting quality problems, sales dropping, 20 percent of the workforce suddenly made redundant and the rest feeling insecure.

I have seen two main obstacles to the composting approach in organizations. One is the reluctance of key individuals. Phil Morris at Alibi Publishing, described in Chapter 3, admitted to me: "I have one speed, and that's fast forward." He did not have the patience or the skills to slow down and compost the fertile mess of divergent views, dissatisfactions, or setbacks. The other obstacle is that the culture and habits of many companies institutionalize waste suppression. A performance culture can easily be a pretext for ignoring the deeper issues: when results go off plan, pressure is applied simplistically to push them back on plan, instead of understanding and using the divergent influence. It is much like the way an intensive farm suppresses the weeds instead of learning from them and using them.

Human energy waste is one of the biggest potential energy sources for an organization. There are also many other forms of corporate waste that can be composted. One is failure: a job assignment that didn't work out, a product launch that failed, a project that is abandoned. It takes resilience and patience to acknowledge and explore such setbacks, but they can be a valuable source of fertile humus to improve performance.

Virosoft

Virosoft had all the signs of a successful company: office lights burning until 9 pm, flashy cars out front, marriages seething, and people suddenly becoming ill. I had been asked to work with the executive board to improve their effectiveness as a team and ease the organization's growth pains. Virosoft has a highly profitable niche in the software business for virus checkers. It was my first experience of a firm doubling in size each year.

The company was the brainchild of Aziz Khan, a brilliant and charming software engineer in his mid-thirties. He had come to the UK from Pakistan to do a doctorate in computer science and started Virosoft in 1993, when he was still only 31. As I got to know Aziz, I could see that his complex character had both blessed and cursed the company. He integrated three different aspects. First, he was likable and approachable: he saw

Virosoft as a family and he lived it. People of all ages and at all levels talked of him as being like a brother. Aziz was also a technical genius: he had created and patented a breakthrough in virus checkers, under the nose of far larger competitors. His third strand was a natural commercial awareness. He came from a family of merchants and traders and his instinct for the customer opportunity was superb. He cheerfully admitted that he supervised the finances by watching the cash balance, as if he were running a market stall, but it worked.

The unhappy family

In the first three years, Virosoft had grown from 6 people to 14, to 30, then to 60. During this time, Aziz was able to provide the necessary linkages himself. By 1997, the organization was expanding as planned from 60 to 130 people and Aziz was busy with international growth. At this stage, when my colleague Gill and I met them, everyone was frustrated. People diverged in their views of the problems and potential solutions, but the sense of confusion and "stuckness" was pretty universal.

Aziz hated conflict. On a one-to-one level he could charm his way through it, but he suppressed any debate at board meetings. He had no idea how to lead an unhappy family, let alone one this size. After our groundwork, Gill and I met with him alone. It took some tough talking, and frequent reminders about the profit problems, to persuade him to face these issues with the board. Over half of Virosoft's whole team were engineers. As Gill and I considered how to create a common language for the company, we felt it needed both technical rigor and human content. We decided to use Myers-Briggs, one of the leading psychometric tests, since it would provide objective measurement and description of differences in personality.

In our first workshop with the executive board, our aim was simply to start creating openness, safety, and understanding. We had already debriefed and coached each director on their own profile. In the workshop, we did not name individuals but we showed the team their collective picture. For example, of the twelve of them, seven were mainly thinking led, five were feeling led. Six preferred a structured approach, six a fluid and pragmatic approach. Eight judged themselves mainly by their own internal standards, four by others' views of them. We emphasized that there were no value judgments in these classifications: it was not better to be one type or other, they were simply different.

The effect of this analytical clarity was like warm sun on frozen ground. The mood of the group lightened and opened. Individuals started to disclose their own profiles. There were laughing exchanges across the table, as different types understood the reasons for previous misunderstandings.

It was in the second workshop that we initiated a composting process within the team. To maintain the air flow, to give overall shape and purpose, we anchored the session on the needs of the business. We had observed that generally the waste issues, the problems, were being ignored. Individual directors were doing their own thing, tackling the urgent not the essential, or escaping on overseas trips. We asked each of them to come to the meeting with a list of their nine most important issues: three for the whole business, three for their department, and three for their own work. We deliberately didn't ask them to bring solutions: we wanted to stoke up the sense of frustration as the fuel for deeper change.

At the start of the workshop, Mumtaz, the finance director, raised a question: "If some of our issues involve a disagreement with someone else here, do you want us to explore them?"

"You mean, is it OK to acknowledge conflicts between you?" I replied.

"Yes." There was a tense silence. Everyone looked at Aziz.

Aziz paused, sighed, and then spoke out. "Look, chaps, you know I can't stand conflict. To be honest, I feel sick at the prospect of sitting here with you openly disagreeing with each other." He shook his head and sighed again. "I know Alan and Gill believe we're stuck because we won't face differences. I guess we can't resolve them till we face them. So, yes, I do want you to acknowledge the conflicts. We're just going to have to trust each other. I mean, that's how it should be in a family." He reached out and grasped the hands of the colleagues on each side of him. Suddenly we had a circle of hands all round the table, and the alchemy had begun.

The negative brainstorm

Gill and I encouraged the team to treat this as a brain dump, a kind of negative brainstorm. We asked them to name their issues and own their feelings about them. "If you have feelings towards a colleague here," I said, "express them, even if they're negative. The one ground rule I ask you to follow is to speak in 'I' not 'you' statements. To say 'I feel angry and let down by you' is your opinion, to which you're always entitled. To tell someone 'you're annoying and unreliable' is a foul, so avoid it."

"And another thing," Aziz put in. "I want you to treat me as one of the team for this session. If you've got a conflict with me, tell me. Just because I couldn't stand it before, don't hold back from arguing with each other now." He grinned, and held up a hand. "I've still got a few nails left to chew."

After that, the heap gathered rapidly. We asked people to voice issues as they arose. This enabled them to start with the easier issues and voice the emotive ones as they felt safer. Gill and I appreciated them, urged them to voice their feelings, and threw in a dash of reason or purpose as needed to keep us on track. Often the response Gill or I gave to issues was analytical. We wanted to encourage the directors themselves to be observant and relate their problems to the needs of the business. We knew that a group of 12 people, mostly new to voicing or responding to strong feelings about their work, would find this process powerful and difficult. We chose to err on the side of safety, even if the compost did not reach peak heat this time. Sometimes we needed to fuel the fire, but more often we showed the others how to manage it.

At one point Salim Hussain, the technical director, got quite angry about his conflicting goals. He pointed at Andrew Holloway, the sales director, and at Aziz. "You two have pushed me into an impossible situation, and I'm damn well sick of it."

"Will you spell out what's upsetting you, Salim?" I asked.

"For one thing, you"—he nodded at Aziz—"tie me down with all these clever calculations. Engineer man-weeks, project time-weeks. You pin my bonus and appraisal on completing the development projects on time."

Aziz spread his hands wide in a peaceable gesture. "But Salim, you agreed all that with me. Where's the problem?"

Salim almost sneered at him. "I suppose you think that's all we do in my group, develop new software? Well it's not. Because you"—he turned on Andrew—"are always on my back, telling me you need us to give your customers technical support. You have no idea how much time these queries take." He turned to the group. "And as long as Mr. Big Promises keeps putting our name on the line…"

"Hang on, Salim," I intervened. "I can see you're upset, but can you back off calling names? Stay with how it feels for you."

Salim looked at Andrew. "I'm sorry."

Andrew nodded. "It's okay, Salim. We're both taking stick for it."

"Salim," Gill asked, "how much of your department's time is this customer support taking up?"

Salim frowned. "It's over 30 percent."

Aziz exploded: "30 percent of your whole capacity! No wonder you're behind on development projects. Why haven't you raised it before?"

Salim gripped the table tensely. "Look, you don't like conflict, you don't like problems. I'm trying to please everyone, so I just do the best I can."

Trusting my intuition despite my ignorance, I asked: "Are the customer queries mostly on one product?"

Salim looked surprised at the question, but answered. "Yes, they're nearly all on Maxim One."

"And is it certain types of installation?" Andrew asked.

"Sure." Salim was becoming calmer as he moved back into technicalities. "It's the bigger, older installations, hybrids."

Operations director Roger interrupted. "Surely they're using it beyond the spec?" He looked sharply at Andrew. "Have we checked that?"

Andrew colored. "I don't know. I'll certainly see."

"If that's the case, can't we sell them an upgrade?" asked Amir, the HR director.

At this point, I intervened: "I'd like each of you to give me a one-word snapshot of how you're feeling at this point."

"Angry," "tense," "angry," "very cross," "I wish I wasn't here," "overwhelmed," "angry."

"Thank you," I said. "So there's quite a lot of strong feelings and tension in the room. I hope you aren't finding that surprising or alarming, because I certainly don't. You've been doing superbly at handling some highly charged issues, and I really want to show my appreciation of how well you've all dealt with this. At this stage, I'd like to ask you to join with me in attempting a way of harnessing some of this negative energy. Are you willing to try something?"

There were cautious nods. I went on: "This is a short exercise I call stand-up comics. The aim is to get the tension moving and start composting it into positive energy. Can you all stand up, please? Now, let your body stretch, ease the tense parts. And try making some funny faces and a few sounds, it all helps to get the energy moving. Aziz will show you how."

Aziz leapt to the challenge and soon they were all groaning, grimacing, and laughing at each other. The atmosphere in the room eased dramatically.

"Excellent," I said. "And now, stand tall, with your knees relaxed, and take some really long, deep breaths, right down into your stomach. Imagine you're breathing right into your tension, and on the out breath imagine the tension becoming a positive flow of energy, up your spine and through your brain. Try the principle of 'don't get mad, get moving.' Imagine how you want to use this energy productively: let's put it into the business of this session."

As we moved the workshop on to solutions, the level of participation and the quality of people's interactions were impressive to all of us.

After this workshop, I questioned Salim: "Were you intending to discuss your workload in that session?"

He shook his head, smiling gently. "No, no. It's not in my culture and it's never been in Aziz's, till now. I've always kept my rubbish in the bin: showing it to colleagues just gives them ammunition. But today, I was somehow carried along by the heat of the group and I'm glad."

Over a period of months, we brought the principles of open communication and composting into the Virosoft culture. Initially our focus was on Aziz and his team, combining one-on-one coaching sessions and a series of group workshops, where we addressed business issues, team dynamics, and the link between them. As the new skills and cycles took root with the directors, we moved on to run cross-functional, three-day workshops that included every manager and supervisor. The first evening of each workshop was a composting session, which we invited one or two directors to attend. The energy and the information released in these sessions were tremendous and the benefits continued long after the workshops.

Methods and processes

Although the habits and processes of conventional organizations may perpetuate waste suppression, there are processes that can develop composting skills and help the habit to take root. Here are some examples:

❖ Training in assertiveness and conflict-resolution skills.
❖ Using a facilitator to help a team process waste energy issues, as in the Virosoft case. Ideally, this should be combined with individual coaching sessions to develop and practice the relevant interpersonal skills.
❖ The creation of peer support groups as a way of learning relevant skills off-line and providing mutual support to apply them.
❖ Establishing forums for open space, two-way dialogue both vertically and horizontally through the organization.
❖ Telephone support lines and face-to-face sessions with independent counselors.
❖ An "all hands" meeting: periodic gatherings of everyone who works in the organization. While these are sometimes used only for top-down messages, they are more productive but less predictable if open questioning and debate are encouraged.

Composting in Daily Practice

As you can probably see, the first three principles of *The Natural Advantage* are interdependent. You need to start cultivating your ground condition and converting to natural energy in order to compost your waste effectively. Recycling requires a number of new habits. The first is to notice and gather waste, instead of ignoring it and pushing it away. The Personal Energy Audit in Chapter 3 can help you to locate your waste, as can the guidelines earlier in this chapter.

The toolkit in Chapter 11 includes two methods that can help you with composting: Connected Breathing, and a valuable tool for changing unhelpful patterns, Negative Energy Recycling.

As you start to gather your waste, you should find that some of it recycles almost instantly, without the need for a composting process. Simply noticing and naming a problem can be enough to show you how to use it. Many types of natural waste can be reabsorbed by fertile ground, so as you develop your clean energy sources and underlying vitality, you can reuse more waste without conscious effort.

6
Organic
Synergy

The organic way is not about forcing output, nor about leaving nature to take its course: it is about harnessing and shaping natural resources and processes to grow value. The key to this is what I call co-creativity: the art of creating output with natural forces, instead of overriding them. Working co-creatively means integrating apparently conflicting qualities, such as push and flow, activity and receptiveness, the planned and the unexpected. By combining these apparent opposites we can find the "gift in the problem," the synergy of uncertainty.

The idea of bringing polarities—apparently opposing qualities—together in our work is not a new concept. For example, the "both/and" approach, being both active and receptive, is something we are now familiar with. However, co-creativity is more like multiplication than addition: $A \times B$, not just $A + B$. It is the process of integrating opposing qualities that cultivates the synergy between them.

Synergy is when one and one equal three: when you use a

problem to move you to a more fruitful outcome. The root meaning of synergy is "energy together" and it is a characteristic of natural growth: by combining energies, the whole is greater than the parts. The idea that the output can be greater than the inputs may seem contradictory, but in natural processes the quality, the usable energy of the output, can far exceed that of the inputs. This helps to explain how organic synergy regenerates resources: composting and soil life are two examples of this.

Many organizations still try to sanitize uncertainty, to push it out of the picture. They seek to control people and events, to achieve results by a preordained plan. This mechanistic approach is exhausting for the people involved and cannot continue to deliver results in a world as changeable as ours. It is especially tough on the leaders, who are expected to know how to fix every new challenge to the plan.

Co-creativity offers a sustainable alternative. Organic farmers produce results amid more uncertainty and with less control than any other managers I know. This requires such skills as observation, humility, and inventiveness, along with traditional management qualities like drive and intelligence. The co-creative approach is like sailing a yacht, not driving a powerboat. It's an art and a process, as well as a technique. And it's not easy to learn it just from a book. For this reason I have included two longer case histories in this chapter to illustrate the concept in practice.

Dirk Hoostra

Dirk is the farmer who converted Magdalen to organic methods. When he joined us in 1991, he was a painful example of macho management. Our situation was like the mad leading the myopic as I attempted to manage Dirk in setting up an organic farm from scratch, but it forced us both to learn fast about co-creativity. Dirk had never been to the UK when he telephoned me from the Netherlands to enquire about the job. He and his partner Marika booked a one-way ticket to England and stayed for three years. As soon as I met Dirk I felt he was right for the farm, but I suspected it would be a tough ride for all of us.

Dirk was 30 years old, a tall, big, red-faced Dutchman. He was fearsomely strong, in physique and in will. His iron drive was invaluable but also caused a lot of problems. Dirk had worked on organic farms and run an organic market garden, but he had no formal training and had never managed a whole farm, let alone started one. And we were literally at ground zero. We had the fields and a few buildings but no tractors, no equipment, no livestock.

Dirk spoke English like a mouthwash, rolling the words around his mouth and spitting them out. He and I liked, respected, and annoyed each other. We were both good at being the charging bull: dominating the situation, imposing our will, making things happen. So Magdalen drove the two of us crazy: trying to push forward with so little understanding or control. How do you buy a cow? What do you do when your wheat crop is full of weeds? We were both so inexperienced that we hardly knew where to start.

The raging bull

For the first few weeks, Dirk raged like a penned bull. He was furious at the problems of getting the farm set up, furious at me and at the British in general.

"Alan, I never was in such a shit situation like this," he told me. "In the market garden in Holland, my boss, he was this rich guy, you know? Everything new, German, runs perfect. And the market garden, was going eight years before I come. I just followed the rules, and it works."

It only took us one phone call to the nearest tractor dealer to discover that buying new equipment for Magdalen was way beyond our budget. "I'm sorry, Dirk," I said. "We'll have to find our way through this together. I guess you'd better try the farm sales." These are the auctions of equipment and stock at a farm that is being sold. It took us into the world of conventional farming, but there seemed no choice.

After a couple of forays, the raging bull was even angrier and hurt too: Dirk took me into the yard to show me the baler he had just bought from a farm sale. He had jacked up one side. "See this?" he asked. "They just fix the drive chain with wire. First time you use it on a field, it breaks. These shits must think I'm a joke. They just make a fool of me." He was fuming, but close to tears.

"I'm really upset by this too, Dirk," I said. "We'd better have a talk with Norman Hale." Norman was a long-established organic farmer nearby, who had been a helpful friend when the Wessex Foundation was buying Magdalen Farm. As Dirk told his tale, Norman shook his head and frowned.

"Something doesn't stack up here," Norman said. "You might think it'd be the law of the jungle at a farm sale, but it isn't. Leastways, not if you treat them right. Shall we do the next one together?"

Treating them like muck

Two weeks later there was a major sale near Yeovil, including several items we needed. It was a daunting scene. A field full of equipment and farmers, most of whom seemed to know each other, and the conversations around the equipment were beyond the ken of Dirk or me. Norman turned to him. "To start with, Dirk, have a go the way you've been doing it. I'll stand by and listen."

Dirk checked his catalog, and walked up to the farmer selling the equipment. He was talking to someone else, but Dirk simply interrupted. "Hey, you got this muckspreader. Does it work good?"

The farmer, clearly surprised, nodded. "Yes..."

"So you don't sell me no shit?" Dirk asked. "No problems, eh?"

"Well, it's in pretty fair order, I'd say..." the farmer began.

"Okay." Dirk ticked his catalog and walked away. We came over and joined him.

Now it was Norman who was upset. "Dirk, you talk about them treating you like muck. That's how you treated him. Is this how you do it in Holland?"

Dirk was open mouthed. "Yeah. What the hell do you mean, I treat him like shit? I just ask him a couple of questions. That's normal, no?"

Norman shook his head. "Look, if you sell something to a mate, you don't screw them, right? You need to make friends with this bloke. Take your time, make it personal. Understand him. Get him talking about his farm."

"You think I have time to think about his farm?" Dirk was getting angry.

Norman stared back at him keenly. "If you want to learn about farming in Dorset, you'd better find the time. I mean, your trouble, both of you, is you don't even know what questions to ask. Yes, get him talking. And make sure you listen."

"Hey, I listen OK." Dirk's face was fiery red by now.

Norman shook his head. "Nonsense. You just fired questions and interrupted him. I mean, let him say what he wants, let him ramble, and the facts you need will come out. Hear his story, and tell your own."

"Tell my story?" Dirk was baffled. "I just need..."

Norman leaned towards him. "Actually, you have a pretty interesting story to tell: coming from abroad and trying to start a farm from scratch. I mean, you really need help. And if you tell your story, you'll start getting it."

I could see Dirk's expression change. Something in him relaxed. He was finally hearing the message.

"Come on, we'll try it out," Norman continued. "You can meet a couple of the farmers I know here."

"OK," Dirk said stiffly. "But there's still something I worry about."

"Go on," I said, "tell us."

"Well, I think these English people see me, they see this big Dutch guy, and they think what a stupid asshole. I think they laugh at me."

Norman laughed, and took him by the shoulder. "Dirk, honestly, it's you that believes that. If you treat them right, they'll treat you right. Just relax."

After that sale, Dirk virtually collapsed. He could see that his rigid, hard-driving mode was not successful or appropriate. He despaired. He fell ill, for the first time in years. First Marika and I had to persuade him to stop. Then we had to coax him to start again. Dirk gradually realized that we wouldn't call him a jerk if he didn't get things right first time. He found that he could look foolish and make mistakes, and still survive.

Columbus style

For several months after the farm sale I saw Dirk veering between attack and despair, but something different was emerging. His hard side was becoming gentler and the soft side was gaining strength. He and I coined the term "Columbus style" for this new approach. We were sitting on the lawn beside the farmhouse, enjoying a sunny early evening in September.

"You know, this is pretty funny, you and me," Dirk said. "We're tough guys, we're like marines, yeah? You give us a map, we go anywhere."

I smiled. "Sure, if we only knew where to go, we'd storm our way to it."

"So with this crazy farm, we don't have a destination." Dirk started to laugh. "You know the trouble, we're off the map, right?"

I nodded. "It's like Christopher Columbus. We're beyond the known world, sailing west…"

He grinned. "Yeah, the crew is nervous, the boat leaks, we might die before we find land…"

"It's running on faith, Dirk," I said. "At least now, we know that we don't know."

Dirk's biggest achievement at Magdalen Farm was starting the dairy herd from scratch in 1992. He bought the livestock, built the facilities, and set up the routines. I only realized the scale of this feat a year later, when I was visiting a leading organic farm in Sweden. When I told Karl, the farmer, what we had done, he actually called his neighbors over so they could see me. "Look at this guy," Karl said, "they just started a dairy herd." They stared at me as if I had walked on the moon. Karl went on, "You don't just start a dairy herd. You need a lot of experience. It takes years."

Dirk's approach to starting the dairy herd was co-creative: he was a very different man from the raging bull at the farm sales a year before. Now, he showed subtlety, ingenuity, and immense patience. It took patience with the cows, but even more with the authorities, who had to approve the milking parlor for health and hygiene.

The standards inspector was suspicious at first: cynical about organics, and seeing us as a bunch of amateurs. He began by telling us that our plans were impossible and unacceptable, throwing the rule book at us. Far from getting angry, Dirk met him with a kind of youthful charm. He spent time explaining what the project was about, and eventually the inspector was so supportive that he sketched out a design for us and explained how to do it economically.

Learning from Agnes

A few weeks after milking had started, I arrived at Magdalen Farm to find Dirk still in the dairy parlor long after he should have finished. He was sitting in a stall with one of the cows, massaging her teat. "What's up?" I asked. I was struck by how peaceful Dirk looked, with his head leaning against the cow's flank.

Very gently, he moved his head, signaling me to come nearer. "I talk to you later," he murmured. "If I talk now, I don't be with the cow."

I went to the farmhouse kitchen. Marika explained to me, "We have a cow with mastitis."

I winced. Mastitis is one of the main threats in organic dairy herds. It is an infection of the udder that is painful for the cow and affects milk quality. One reason conventional dairy herds are dosed with antibiotics is to avoid mastitis, although this creates a number of other problems. When Dirk came in, I could see he was tired and distressed. "I just don't know if it's working," he said. "We have to wait till morning, then we know."

"Did you get the vet in?" I asked.

Dirk nodded. "Sure. He told me to use antibiotics. I said to him…"

"But hang on," I interrupted. "If you do that, the milk's not organic grade. I mean, surely we…"

"Hey, hey, Alan. Relax." He put a hand on my shoulder and smiled. "You don't let me finish. You don't listen enough!" He laughed. "We don't use antibiotics, not yet, anyway. I talk also to Norman. He tells me how they do it with no drugs. That's why I massage the teat. See, it helps the circulation, and that helps to fight the disease."

"We also use a homeopathic remedy we get from Norman," Marika added. "The vet says it's okay to try, but he comes in two days: if Agnes isn't right then, we have to give her antibiotics."

"Congratulations, Dirk," I said. "So Jongheer Columbus becomes an expert on massaging cows. You're turning into quite a learner."

In the end, Agnes had to be treated with antibiotics. "We were too slow to see the problem," Dirk explained to me. "It pisses me off, but we just didn't have the experience."

A few weeks later, at one of our progress meetings, Dirk said, "You know, the mastitis problem with Agnes really teach us a lot. I tell you what we do after that."

I nodded. "How did it help?"

"After that, Marika and me, we were so upset, you know? We said, we don't ever want this problem again."

"Isn't that a bit tough on you?" I asked.

Marika spoke. "Maybe, but it really makes us think. It's like, we start milking, we do it OK, but this makes us want to do it really good."

"So what we do," Dirk went on, "is we go to Norman's farm, and we shadow his dairyman. Two times we go there, both of us, and we watch everything. Now, we know what we look for. Lots of things about hygiene, you know? And we learn about stress."

Put yourself in their hoofs

This was a new idea for me. "Really? Stress for cows?" I asked guardedly.

He nodded enthusiastically. "You think: we buy these cows out of three different herds. They don't know each other, it's hard for them."

Marika added, "We have five cows who all try to be boss. They all push to be the first one into the milking parlor."

I shook my head. "So what do we do about stress in cows? Run a team-building workshop?"

Dirk laughed. "Well, Marika and I just put ourselves in their hoofs. We pretend we're the cows, and we don't like how this loud Dutch guy treat us. Now I don't push them around so much. I don't swear at them no more. And we give each cow more space." It was winter, so the cows were housed indoors, on straw. "We move some cows to the second barn. And we make it more easy: we give them extra straw for the last four weeks. That don't cost us much, and already they give something back."

"What do you mean, give something back?" I asked.

Dirk grinned. "The yield goes up. More milk each day."

I have described Dirk's progress at length because it shows how co-creativity can develop. When Dirk came to Magdalen, he only had one response to problems: to narrow his focus and push. It didn't produce lasting satisfaction for him or the problems. While you move toward sustainability, you have no choice but to learn co-creativity. As Dirk's experience shows, the tensions of trying to achieve results without control or clarity can help to teach you how.

Dirk's drive pushed him to keep facing the problems, and slowly he started to integrate active and receptive skills. He learned when to push and when to yield. And he gained the crucial habit of relaxing into a problem, exploring it observantly, instead of tensing and forcing. The result was that he created organic synergy out of a series of difficulties. The way Dirk handled the farm sales, the dairy parlor, and the mastitis all took us further forward than we could have hoped for. In each case, he eventually found the gift in the problem.

I often find that external issues are enlarged reflections of my internal ones. Dirk's raging-bull style showed me my own tendency to push too hard. The finesse in receptive skills he developed, and the way he combined this with determination, taught me a great deal. I also learned from the way his partner, Marika, changed while at Magdalen. At first, she was too passive to be co-creative. What she had to learn was how and when to push.

Part of my own payback from the mastitis problem came months later, when Phil Morris asked me to "clean up" the newly formed customer support group at Alibi Publishing, described in Chapter 3. "We've got the mother of all bottle-necks down there, Alan," Phil said, fuming. "It's clogging the whole bloody system. If they can't sort it, I'll go through them like a dose of salts, so help them." This sounded like the anti-biotic option, so I tried Dirk's gentler methods. For the cus-tomer support group this meant giving space, support, and attention, disclosing the real problems. It also meant taking the pressure off and rebuilding their vitality so that they could work the problems out for themselves.

Organic Synergy on the Farm

"We have been growing herb plants for over 15 years now, start-ing with a few excess plants from our own garden ... We had invented our own growing medium, peat-based with concreting sand, calcified seaweed and ... composted municipal waste as the nutrient source. By some miracle this gave acceptable results and we were able to start slowly expanding the sale of plant pro-duction ... The range of varieties we grow now numbers about 400 ... We have tried as many different organic growing media as we can get hold of ... pests and diseases are not a great prob-lem. The rusts which plague conventional chemical herb grow-ers just do not seem to appear." (Profile on Alex and Hilary Duthie in *New Farmer & Grower* magazine, 1996)

You won't find the words synergy and co-creativity on organic farmers' lips, nor in their handbooks. Yet the approach is fundamental to their ability to work with nature. Kahu, the teacher I met in Hawaii, urged me not to box him up or pin him down, not to dissect living wisdom into a list of techniques. In the same way, the co-creativity of the organic farmer can't be reduced to a formula: it is more like the quality of good ground condition, a living organism with natural vitality and adaptability.

Traditionally, farming skills have been passed from generation to generation. The young farmer learned a mass of information and skills by experience, living with the cycles of the land for years. Then came modern, intensive farming, what Peter Norman calls recipe farming: "You just call up your feed and chemical suppliers, and they send you a mix. The last thing Monsanto and the big boys want a farmer to do is think creatively; they want to be paid for that."

Although organic farming builds on traditional methods, much of it has to be reinvented. For one thing, there are new pollutants, pests, and weather conditions. And as Dirk used to tell me, "Every piece of land is different. You have to live with a farm for years before you understand it right." The area of land in Britain farmed organically grew tenfold between 1985 and 2000 and many of those coming into organic farming didn't have the benefit of growing up in farming families and acquiring years of experience. Add to this the variety of food consumers now demand and the range of distribution channels, and you'll see why they had to learn fast.

All farms have to cope with major uncertainties, but their responses can be very different. The conventional farmer seeks to turn a fluid, natural system into an artificial, mechanical one. By controlling the inputs of fertility and suppressing problems, he tries to regulate the situation and impose a predictable result.

This has uncomfortable echoes of total quality assurance, business process reengineering, and other schemes that often seek to sanitize the messiness of real life and codify it into orderly but artificial stability. The trouble is, you usually need mess to create synergy.

The incidents I have described with Dirk Hoostra are typical of the organic way. By staying with the mess of setback and uncertainty, you reach a synergistic solution: one that addresses root causes, not symptoms, harvesting the learning from the problem. Weeds and pests are a good example of this. An organic farm may seem to be vulnerable because it doesn't use chemicals to suppress them. In practice, a cultivated natural system will keep the problems in manageable proportions. The biological activity in healthy soil is resistant to threats, just as a healthy person's immune system prevents infection taking root. Weeds and pests will be present, but they don't take over. It may look messy, but the problems also serve a purpose: they actually contribute to the resilience and productivity of the land. And the organic farmer uses them for feedback, adjusting the system as necessary.

The equivalent to this for you and your work is to cultivate your natural resilience and trust your full array of talents, instead of relying on logic to master every problem. If you can relax into uncertainty and cultivate receptive observation, synergy will be able to emerge, whether through intuition, emotional intelligence, inspiration, or gut feel.

Organic Synergy: Exploring the Principle

My experience of teaching co-creativity and synergy is that the concepts are understandable and attractive, but elusive for most people. Each of the following is vital for achieving synergy:

❖ Building up creative tension: exploring, facing, and feeling the intensity of two or more apparently conflicting aspects of a situation.

❖ Staying with the tension and relaxing into it.

❖ Applying both intuitive and analytical tools, such as creative conflict resolution, to explore the tensions further and open a way to potential outcomes.

❖ Using a range of creativity-building methods to stimulate insights and ideas that may provide the solution.

This section describes some of its main ingredients using creative tension, the whole brain, and working vision. The Diamond Process applies this approach, as do other methods covered in Chapter 11.

Creative tension

The ability to meet high levels of uncertainty positively is central to the remarkable resilience of organic farmers. The co-creative response to tension, uncertainty, or contradictory data is to explore it and relax into it. You can play with the tension, make a joke of it, as I did by hamming up my frustration and doing my Groucho Marx act in the incident described in Chapter 5. Although the idea of relaxing into tension may feel strange, it is taught in many eastern philosophies. Buddhist meditation masters will suggest that you witness your tensions, and breathe into them. Tantra, the Indian approach to aligning sexuality and spirituality, teaches that the fullest ecstasy arises when we let go into a high state of arousal, riding the tension instead of discharging it.

The nature of a co-creative process means that we cycle between the polarities or extremes, we repeatedly immerse ourselves in each of them. We develop strength, creative tension, and the potential for integration by moving between them. The synergistic quality arises because we deliberately use and harness the tension to move us forward.

Drawing on both sides of the brain

One way of understanding and developing co-creativity is through the left and right sides of the brain. Roger Sperry, an American psychologist, won the Nobel prize for medicine in 1981 for his research on the different characteristics of the left and right hemispheres of the human brain. The talents of the left side include logic, verbal and numerical reasoning: the ability to analyze a complex situation, to dissect it into parts, to identify linear chains of cause and effect. Many people would see such skills as the sum total of mental ability, but this is only half the story.

The right side of the brain offers such gifts as intuition and imagination: it is more visual, spatial, and conceptual. While the left brain can dissect a complex situation, break it into smaller parts by analysis, it is the right side that gives us synthesis, creative vision, the fresh combination of parts to move us forward.

The right and left sides of the brain equate to the archetypal feminine and masculine qualities, which Chinese philosophy calls yin and yang. The yin, feminine, includes receptive, yielding, intuitive, unconscious, and integrating qualities. The yang, or masculine, includes active, conscious, penetrating, rational, testing, and distinguishing or separating qualities. Most people habitually use one of these sets of qualities—one side of the brain—more than the other. Yet all of us have the potential to develop and integrate both. Doing so raises our energy productivity, our adaptability, and our co-creativity.

Working vision

American president George Bush may be best remembered for his admission that "I'm no good at this vision thing." The debate has been running for years over the importance of vision and how to achieve it. Much of the confusion arises from conflict between left-brain and right-brain approaches, and the failure to realize that a working vision includes and integrates both sides.

Sustainable success requires vision and clarity in both everyday operations and overall strategy. The way to achieve this is by combining focused and peripheral vision, which equate to the active/left brain and receptive/right brain. They also represent two of the main schools of thought regarding "the vision thing." The left-brain approach to vision sees it as deduced from analysis: objectively assessing capabilities, opportunities, and stakeholder needs. The vision is then logically cascaded into a strategy and action plans. By contrast, the right-brain approach sees vision as creative and inspirational: it arises intuitively from those involved, from their picturing the qualities of the desired future. The most viable and appropriate visions arise from integrating these two approaches. For example, Dirk Hoostra created a productive dairy herd at Magdalen by integrating driving ambition with observation of details.

Think about your own typical ways of exploring a situation. Is your way of seeing driven by your desired outcomes, so you home in quickly on the details you judge to be important? Or is your typical way of looking soft-focused, receptive, scanning the scene for the information that presents itself?

Whether you favor the focused or peripheral approach, cultivate both types of vision, alternate between them, and then seek to combine them. While the concept of the left and right sides of the brain may still seem abstract, noticing and cultivating these two ways of seeing is a practical way to develop them.

All the visioning methods I use involve the breath in some way. At minimum, they all begin with some slow, relaxing breaths to engage the air element more fully. The specific methods include:

❖ *Meditation*: sitting in silence, focusing on the breath, opening receptively to clarity and direction.

❖ *Visualization*: a range of guided journeys, often in natural
settings, to explore a situation, face and release negative feelings, reach a vision, and integrate it into practicality.

❖ *Vision questing*: a process found in the Celtic, Native
American, and other traditions. It involves spending time
alone, in an isolated natural setting, calling for your vision,
and finding guidance and support from your surroundings.

The Diamond Process

The Diamond Process offers a route map for the co-creative
approach. I developed this process as a way of teaching managers how to handle high levels of change and uncertainty syn-
ergistically. It is relevant for issues that are mainly practical,
mainly emotional, or mainly inspirational. It can be applied
quickly or in depth.

The shape of the diamond symbolizes the shape of most
change processes. There is a starting point: an intention, a question, or a partial understanding of the situation. From this
point, the picture widens into growing uncertainty, confusion,
and contradiction. A successful change process then finds new
insight that gives clarity and focus, bringing the process to a finishing point, which in turn will typically be the start of another
diamond.

The six stages in the process are as follows.

Intent

You plant the seed for this process by stating and affirming your
intent. Even if your aim is as vague as "to understand my confusion," it helps to state this explicitly. Feeling your tension and
affirming your desire to reach an outcome raise your energy and

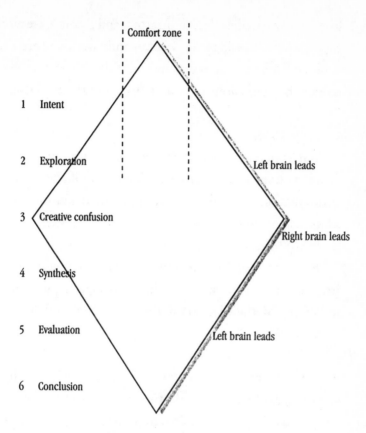

Figure 8 The Diamond Process

motivation for the process. Another benefit of doing all this is that it engages your subconscious and unconscious mental capacities in the process. The same approach is expounded by Timothy Gallwey in *The Inner Game of Tennis*: the conscious brain specifies the goal, but never prescribes how to achieve it. It briefs the unconscious mind to find the solution.

Exploration

In each phase of the Diamond Process, both sides of the brain contribute but one takes the lead. Here it is the active, logical, left brain. This is the stage for gathering data, exploring a wide range of information sources, analyzing what's going on, looking for parallels, lead indicators, and so on. One aim of the exploration phase is to go well beyond your comfort zone: the habitual frame of reference and limiting beliefs that we use to reduce the confusions of real life to a manageable level.

Creative confusion

If your exploratory work has been done well, it will naturally propel you into confusion. Real life is full of changeability and contradiction, to an extent that can be almost intolerable. As TS Eliot said, "Humankind cannot bear very much reality." The word confusion literally means a flowing together, and the aim in this stage is to relax into the tension and uncertainty: to feel its intensity and to stay with it. This stage is the transition to leadership by the right brain, the receptive principle.

Synthesis

This is the phase when you open receptively to the "aha!" moment, the creative insight that produces a way forward from the creative confusion. Like any right-brain process, you can't force it. There is a saying, "In sleep, sex and fishing, the more you try, the less happens." The same applies here. Sometimes just closing your eyes, breathing peacefully, and waiting enables you to find the synergy. If not, this is a good time to go for a walk, have a bath, make a meal, play some music: do something enjoyable and stay observant for the answer when it's ready. If you want a specific method for this stage, try the Witness Triangle, described in Chapter 11.

Evaluation

This is where the left brain takes the lead again. You have a vision of an outcome: it may seem obvious or crazy. Either way, you need to check out the practicalities, do the sums, ask the awkward questions, understand the implications. Few of us have 100 percent infallible intuition, and you may have to return to an earlier phase of the cycle.

Conclusion

Your evaluation may wholly support your new vision or highlight doubts or risks. Before you go ahead, return to the right brain: sit with your potential decision, see it in perspective, ask if it inspires and motivates you. This is the stage we often include before an important decision by saying: "I'll sleep on it."

It is sometimes appropriate to cycle back within this process and repeat some stages. For example, confusion may raise more questions to explore. Or you may alternate for a while between confusion and synthesis. It is also cyclical because the conclusion to one diamond often becomes the starting point for another.

Dancing with Worms: Lumex USA

In 1983, at the age of 35, I achieved my ambition of becoming a managing director. However, the business involved was hardly a star prize. Redland Lumex, the division I was to run, was like a couple of small, scruffy, leaking tramp steamers. It sat awkwardly alongside Redland's bigger divisions, which were like cruise liners: upmarket, smooth, and profitable.

Peter Jansen had interviewed me and turned me down as managing director of Redland Bricks, a job I dearly wanted. He was disarmingly frank about Lumex: "I know you'd like to run a business where you can be creative with the marketing and product design. This isn't it. Quite honestly, we know Lumex USA is a mess, but we have no idea how much of one. If you can clean up the can of worms for me, I'll find you something to run that you'll really enjoy."

The Lumex division was an assortment of businesses in road

markings and maintenance. Lumex UK employed 400 people across six different operations. Its profits were good for this sector, but way below Redland's norms. Lumex USA had 200 employees in two divisions, at five locations, and was in its second year of losing money. "My hunch is that the true losses are worse than reported," Peter told me. "I want you to focus on the US and spend as much time as it takes to sort it." I got the commute from Guildford, UK to Chicago, Illinois down to a fine art.

Facing the fog

I started at Lumex with a naive confidence that I could easily manage a turnaround business in America. I had dealt with several loss-making operations in the UK. And with a Harvard MBA, and four years working for Procter and Gamble UK, I thought I knew US culture. In practice, Lumex was a rude shock, a nightmare. In other turnarounds, it had been easy to find the tags—the slack cost controls, the quick sales opportunities—but not here.

At Lumex, my first impression was fog. I couldn't gather any usable facts from the US management's patter. I felt desperately frustrated and eager to act decisively, to be the hero. But I could find neither the sword nor the dragon. The only obvious action was to fire the president of the company. I discussed this with Peter Jansen after my second visit to Lumex USA. "I'm sure he'll have to go," I told Peter, "but not yet. I need two or three people with me who are competent and trustable. I haven't found them yet and I don't have the capacity to take this on alone."

By month four I had found a few people in the business I could entrust with senior roles. It was made hard for me to get to know them fully, so I had to give them trial assignments based on intuition and impressions. Most of these gambles worked well, some failed. And I was clear that my new team were steady-handed operators, not strategists or leaders.

By month six, the operational problems were largely identified and costed. We were producing reliable financial reports and forecasts, but the picture horrified Redland. Losses were running into seven figures and that wasn't the worst of it. The biggest concern, for Redland and for me, was that there was no end in sight. Even after six months, I could not come up with any strategy to make the business profitable. I felt appalled at my failure. Peter Jansen had been completely supportive, but he told me, "You'd better know that there are some senior murmurings around here that you're not up to the job. I know it's been a hell of a time for you, but I'd like you to set a target time for proposing a strategy."

My heart sank. I responded: "How about three months from now?"

Despite my track record, Lumex USA looked hopeless. Its main business was supplying road-marking paint to state highway authorities. These authorities specified the product formula precisely and took the lowest price from sealed bids. Most of the cost was in purchased raw materials. There was almost zero opportunity to add value to sales or to take out costs. The volumes were so large that any diversification would be a drop in the bucket. Competition for these contracts was severe and the profit margins were thin at best. If your material costs or factory yields were even slightly out, you lost money. For these reasons, the business was almost unsalable. Closure was the obvious option, but the shutdown costs were so high that it was better to find a way to keep going.

A crone or a frog

Having committed to my deadline, I felt like the youngest son in so many fairy tales: the foolish youth who undertakes the impossible task. He typically wanders aimlessly, sometimes desperately, until a chance meeting with a crone or a frog solves his problem. Since all my strategic analysis and direct efforts had failed, I decided to go on walkabout. It was not entirely random, but I set forth in a receptive, observant spirit. For once, I did not have lists of sharp questions to ask: I felt this might prevent me from finding the unexpected.

The tension felt unbearable between my desire to push ahead to a solution and the apparent impasse on all fronts. At times I lapsed into my usual ways of avoiding tension: despair or distraction. I would give up, let go, feeling hopeless and overwhelmed. This allowed me to rest and release some of my stress. At other times, I would distract myself by getting busy with simpler tasks that I could achieve. This gave me some diversity in my work, and renewed my vitality. However, most of the time I kept myself in the tension between the active and receptive modes, and it was from this tension that the creative leap emerged.

In the space of three weeks, I revisited all our factories. I also went to meet customers and suppliers. I attended an industry conference and met our competitors for the first time. This had to be approached carefully, because antitrust law was actively enforced and Redland was determined to avoid any hint of price fixing. The seed of a solution came from a titanium dioxide supplier in Pittsburgh. "Of course, Al, the key to your business is freight," he said.

In the past, if someone's views contradicted my prejudices, I found a way to devalue them. I could easily have written this guy off as a has-been full of irrelevant folklore. Not now: I was open to clues. Maybe this was the frog!

I sat up. "Freight? What do you mean?"

Rick pushed his steel-rimmed glasses back up his nose. "Sure. Your product is about the cheapest damn stuff you can buy in a barrel. The cost of trucking goods in and hauling 'em out is a big number. You won't make much profit shipping more than 500 miles from a plant."

After that I could hardly wait to finish the conversation and get hold of a map. There were so few competitors in this game that I could plot every location from memory. Suddenly a picture emerged. I could see that our plant in Tennessee was a no-hoper. The population within 200 miles was quite small. Competitors were better placed for the big markets in Georgia and Texas, whereas Milwaukee looked like a good location. Our problems there were an oversized, antiquated plant and a competitor only 100 miles away.

I can still recall sitting with the map and my concentration drifting. An idea shot through me like a bolt of electricity, startling in its power and simplicity. If we could buy our competitor's plant in Green Bay and simply shut down our old plant in Milwaukee, we would be 800 miles from the nearest competitor. I was pretty sure that the freight costs of competitors would enable us to add a few percent to our profit margin. And so it proved.

I took my ideas to my Lumex USA team, who welcomed them with relief and helped to refine them. Once we had a clear vision of a solution, we went for it like a tornado. The numbers worked. Peter Jansen and Redland gave it their backing. I estimated what our competitor's factory had cost to build, and what it was worth to us, and I drove a good bargain.

Two other finds from my walkabout added to the successful turnaround strategy. One was poaching Anna Santini, the general manager of Beldue, our largest and most successful competitor. Anna was tired of the politics in Beldue's parent company. She liked my enthusiasm and the semi-independence she'd gain from having a boss in the UK. Anna was naturally co-creative. She had superb observation and intuition, but she was tough too. She had a degree in chemistry and had always wanted to manage a factory. To get there she'd had to join as the plant manager's secretary and prove herself at every step. Having her as president of Lumex USA was an immense relief for all of us.

The other breakthrough came from an impulsive decision to attend a Milwaukee Chamber of Commerce dinner. Because we sold over a wider radius, no one had ever bothered to attend. By attending I met the presidents of two other businesses in Milwaukee who were big buyers of the same raw materials. We also realized that our seasonal demand cycles were complementary. It became obvious to pool our purchases and this added several percentage points to our margins.

I had realized on day two of my time with Lumex that it would never be Redland's kind of business. It would have to be sold, but first it had to be salable. The losses in year one were ugly. But from early in year two, Lumex USA returned to profit and I was able to start seeking a buyer. The American business was eventually sold as a management buyout to Anna Santini and the team I had helped to build.

My experience at Lumex, like Dirk Hoostra's at Magdalen Farm, forced me to learn co-creativity. Both of us were determined to achieve sustainable results in a situation we could neither understand nor control. Without toughness, we'd have failed. Without receptiveness and subtlety, we'd never have found a way though. By staying with the tension of uncertainty, the gift in the problem eventually emerged.

Organic Synergy in Organizations

Developing co-creativity is even more beneficial and challenging for groups than for individuals. The culture and dynamics in many work teams inhibit this kind of process. Mechanistic approaches, using controlled inputs to force a predetermined outcome, will promote conformity, however hard they claim to empower.

Some of the leading management thinkers of the past decade have argued for the move toward organic synergy, albeit in different language. One example is Stephen Covey, in *The Seven Habits of Highly Effective People*. His Habit 6: Synergize, offers valuable guidelines and examples on how to apply it in organizations. For example, appropriate reward and recognition systems are an important factor. Covey comments:

"I did some consulting for another company that wanted training for their people in human relations. The underlying assumption was that the problem was the people.

"The president said, 'Go into any store you want and see how they treat you. They're just order takers. They don't understand how to get close to the customers...'

"I persisted, and within two days we uncovered the real problem. Because of the job definition and the compensation system, the managers were 'creaming.' They'd stand behind the cash register and cream all the business during the slow times...

"So the managers would give all the dirty jobs—inventory control, stock work, and cleaning—to the salespeople...

"That's why the department heads were tops in sales.

"So we changed one system—the compensation system— and the problem was corrected overnight. We set up a system whereby the managers only made money when their salespeople made money. We overlapped the needs and goals of the managers with the needs and goals of the salespeople.

"And the need for human relations training suddenly disappeared. The key was developing a true Win/Win reward system."

The Exploration of Chaos and Complexity Theory by Ralph Stacey and others is also relevant. Chaos theory suggests that the most productive, creative, adaptive systems embody "bounded uncertainty": they have processes that can structure and channel fluidity, rather than suppressing it. This is akin to the co-creative notion of integrating the active/structured and receptive/fluid qualities.

In addition, Peter Senge's book *The Dance of Change* overlaps with the co-creative approach, although he uses this term in a narrower sense than I have. For example, he comments that "Leadership grows from the capacity to hold creative tension," and cites Martin Luther King as one example. He reports the views of a number of successful change leaders, which include the importance of persisting receptively amid ambiguity and lack of clarity.

The push and flow culture

Appropriate culture and values are the ground condition in which co-creativity can take root and flourish in an organization. This means fostering values that may seem opposed to each other: for example cooperation with competition, high trust with high challenge, push with flow.

Caradon was a good example of this: there was a strong drive for performance, along with deep willingness to listen, flow, and adapt to achieve it. We created an *esprit de corps* in the group as a whole that balanced rather than swamped the pride people felt for their operating company. Competition and comparison are natural drives, and we harnessed them in encouraging each business and each team to progress. However, we also created processes for collaboration between companies. Several Caradon companies had related product lines and served the same customers. In the past this had just created tension: now, much of this was converted into fruitful synergy.

A co-creative culture is likely to be values led, not results driven. In *Built to Last*, Collins and Porras reveal that only three of the eighteen sustainably successful companies they studied began with a specific product idea. Most developed around values, around the kind of company they wanted to be. This contrast between values-led and results-driven cultures also typifies the difference between organic and intensive farming.

A good example of co-creative culture is given by Bill Hewlett, co-founder of Hewlett-Packard, cited in *Built to Last*:

"When I talk to business schools occasionally, the professor of management is devastated when I say that we didn't have any plans when we started—we were just opportunistic. We did anything that would bring in a nickel. We had a bowling foul-line indicator, a clock drive for a telescope, a thing to make a urinal flush automatically, and a shock machine to make people lose weight. Here we were, with about $500 in capital, trying whatever someone thought we might be able to do."

Another crucial ingredient in the co-creative culture is the willingness to face conflict and resolve it constructively. Consider Virosoft, profiled in Chapter 5. Aziz Khan had built a values-led organization with diverse talents and temperaments. He had assembled the ingredients for highly productive creative tension, but had suppressed them because of his reluctance to face conflict openly. When he signaled his willingness to change and we provided the skills, Virosoft rapidly became a co-creative culture. The business started to find its synergies and improved its results and its resilience in the process.

Propagating the skills

Some of the most frustrated chief executives I meet have a clear vision of future direction. Their problem is that because they can state the vision, they expect the organization to move straight into actioning it. In my experience, culture, skills, and processes all have to evolve before vision and action will align. Although there is an element of alchemy at the heart of co-creative processes, there are a number of skills that can stimulate this alchemy and remove the barriers. These begin with assertiveness: the ability to express, hear, and stay present with emotions. As Thomas Crum says, "In order to have conflict resolution, you've got to have conflict."

Without assertiveness, there is no creative tension, no dialogue to develop: only suppression, blow-ups, or walk-aways. When I led the assertiveness training session for the directors at Alibi Publishing, I was unsure if a busy, hard-nosed senior team would be receptive to it. I was impressed by the eagerness with which they took in and used these methods. Another example is Intel, which runs management classes in "constructive confrontation."

Consider an episode in Philip Carroll's transformational leadership at Shell Oil Company in the USA, quoted in *The Dance of Change*:

"Eighteen months into the process, after a series of regular off-site meetings to talk about our values and plan the transformation together, it began to dawn on the members of the Leadership Council: we didn't have the basic skills to listen to people and let their ideas make an impression on us... We could not even engage ourselves in discussion. Some of us shut down in the face of disagreement. Others tried to win every argument... It took in-depth reflective work and a series of private meetings for us to learn to listen more effectively. As that started to happen, people throughout the organization began to gain confidence in our efforts. I began to hear, for the first time, talk about the process of transformation from people out at offshore drilling base camps, or at refineries."

Processes for uncertainty

The difficulty in describing processes to engender synergy is that they are often nonspecific, and may seem vague. The drive for action and focus in most organizations is so intense that the main need is often to provide space for receptivity. An example is the peer group review process at energy giant BP-Amoco. The 200-plus business units form part of peer groups, and directors from these companies meet in self-facilitated sessions once a year. These provide an open space for exchange of experiences, mutual observation, and identifying the often-subtle cues for an issue that has to be addressed. At the end of each peer group review, the session is joined by a member of BP-Amoco's executive board, so that the experiences and impressions can be transmitted directly.

Processes to cultivate observation, peripheral vision, and receptiveness to soft data can be developed within existing formats. Here is an example from David Marsing, the vice-president, general manager of assembly test manufacturing for Intel, quoted in *The Dance of Change*:

"In staff meetings we'd say, 'How's the factory doing?' Everybody wanted to shoot his hand up with a quantitative indicator. 'No,' I said. 'Don't give me any data. How does it feel on the floor, working with your people? How does it feel to be in some of the key meetings?' The first few times we did this, people looked at me as if to say, 'Where is he coming from?' But we deliberately made it a regular practice—conducted with such repetitiveness that it became integrated into our everyday work life. Then they began to look forward to it. They also began to interact differently with their people. This subtle twist, just a simple little thing, started to get people to exercise their observational skills, and use a different part of their brain...

"I decided to personally practice enough so that I could integrate and embody these skills in myself. This meant establishing a routine of meshing intuitive and analytical behavior, acting and reflecting, listening and advocating, 'task' work and process work, and analytic problem solving and systems thinking, without having to consciously think about it. I now believe that my ability to tap into the organization's potential was a direct result of developing a strong ability to integrate these tools."

Organic Synergy in Daily Practice

What is most important in achieving this quality is a deeply felt understanding of the principles, and the learning skills that enable it. With time, co-creativity becomes a habitual instinct more than a technique. It starts with the basic response to uncertainty: when you feel yourself tensing don't push, don't give up, relax and explore.

The Diamond Process described earlier in this chapter gives you a basic route map for applying co-creativity to generate synergy. The organic growth toolkit in Chapter 11 offers several tools to assist in this process, as well as advice on further reading. These tools include:

❖ *The Witness Triangle*: a simple method using physical movement and visualization to explore two positions that are in tension and find a third point, the synergy that builds on them.

❖ *The Aikido Approach*: pointers from this Japanese martial art based on the principle of using conflicting forces constructively.

❖ *Connected Breathing*: a simple breathing method that can help you relax into tension.

❖ *Creative Conflict Resolution*: a detailed guide to a process that can be useful in finding the synergy in conflicts, either internal or external.

7
Riding the Cycles

Any sustainable system, whether at work or on the farm, will be based on natural cycles, cultivated to achieve productive goals. A cycle is a recurrent succession of things. The root origin of the word is the Greek *kuklos*, meaning circle or wheel, although often a cycle is best pictured as a spiral, since it creates renewable, forward or upward movement, not just repetition. The earth actually gains in vitality by being cycled in the right way. So do batteries. And so do people.

The main benefit of aligning with cycles is to generate high output in a way that is renewing and balancing. Cycles can help us to establish sustainable rhythms in our work, to handle the pressures pulling us towards depletion, and to raise our resilience to change. Without renewal cycles in our work and personal life, it's perfectly possible to dissipate the benefits of clean energy inputs. Have you ever returned from a thoroughly refreshing holiday only to feel that the effect has worn off two weeks later?

The specific cycles that are right for a farm will depend on the desired outputs, soil type, climate, and many other circumstances. In the same way, you need to identify or evolve the specific cycles that are appropriate for your work and your organization.

The cyclicality of the natural world is inescapable. Think of the daily cycle of light and night, the lunar cycle of wax and wane, and the annual cycle of the four seasons. If we turn to consider people at work, some of the trends appear anticyclical. There is the pressure of connectivity: if you are reachable almost every waking hour, on the mobile, by email, by pager, you risk being exposed to the pressure for output almost continually. Likewise, there is a push for longer service hours and 24-hour access in many sectors.

What trends like this make clear is that cyclicality now has to be chosen and consciously created. The pressures toward linear working and depletion won't disappear, but some of the apparent problems can be harnessed to our advantage. Longer hours of service and the explosive growth in communications create scope for us to configure ways of working to match the cycle styles of different individuals.

This chapter offers both the overall principles of working with cycles and specific models to consider. It focuses on three main cycles:

❖ *The cultivation cycle*: including all four seasons in your work patterns: spring—seeding, summer—growth, autumn—harvesting, winter—rest and review.
❖ *Renewal rotation*: applying the principle of crop rotation in your work, so that a demanding task is followed by a restorative one or a fallow period.
❖ *Nutrient cycling*: ensuring that fresh energy nutrients are habitually moved from where they arise to where they are most needed.

Salim Hussain

The technical director of Virosoft, Salim Hussain, met me for monthly individual coaching sessions for over a year. This was part of the program described in Chapter 5. When I arrived at Salim's office for our third session, he looked shocked and dejected. "I've just had my annual medical," he explained. "I have a problem with high blood pressure. And I may be getting ulcers." He laughed bitterly and shook his head. "It's so damn stupid. My wife is a nurse, and she's been telling me for months that I can't go on like this."

"So why can't you go on, Salim?" I asked. "What's dragging you down?"

His face reddened and his hands clenched. "Everything! The job is running me. It's like a treadmill that never stops, in fact it speeds up. If I could... hang on." He darted out to bark instructions at a young engineer who had been peering through the glass partition.

"Would you be willing to try something a little unusual?"

He shrugged. "Why not, nothing to lose, eh?"

"Could you ease up, and relax for a minute? Let your imagination emerge. See if you can recall a time you felt really happy in your work, when you could go on forever." To my surprise, he did lean back, and a dreamy smile came over him.

"Oh yes." He took off his glasses and looked at me. "I was a junior lecturer in computing science at Brunel University."

"Did you enjoy the work?"

Salim sat up proudly. "I was as happy as Larry. I had research funding, was free to do my own projects, and I lectured for 12 hours a week. It all worked beautifully. When I was stuck on research, I'd prepare for a lecture. When I came back to the lab, often my problem was solved."

Forever midsummer

At this point, I took Salim through the four seasons cycle, described in detail later in the chapter. I explained the value of including all four stages: spring—seeding, summer—growth, autumn—harvest, and winter—rest and review. When I had finished, Salim grunted angrily. "Well, my problem's clear. It's forever midsummer in my job. Constant push for output."

"OK," I said, "but who's making it that way? Aziz gives you a lot of freedom and respect, Salim. I challenge you to do things differently."

Salim spluttered, called for a coffee, and started thinking.

"Can you think of work you enjoy in each phase of the cycle?" I asked.

Salim tensed up. "Ah, not in spring, no. I don't like starting projects," he looked at me apologetically. "You see, I'm such a damn perfectionist. That's why I hate giving promises."

Light started to dawn for me. "So that's why Aziz and Andrew always have to chase you to set project timings?"

He nodded, pursing his lips. "Mm. Not good, is it? But summer, growth, if it's the right project, this is what I love."

"What makes it the right project?" I asked.

"If it's real research, something to stretch my brain. It's all these damn people and logistics that get under my skin."

"So what about the autumn, harvest season?" I asked. "Do you like that?"

He looked uncomfortable again. "Frankly, no. I don't want to sign things off until they're 100 percent right. The longer you go on with a piece of software, the more you see how it should be done. Always I have to let it go too soon. My God, if you knew all the little bugs in our programs. I could scream."

I nodded. "I can see that's really hard for you. What about winter, rest and review?"

He suddenly looked sad. "In my academic work, I used to

love this. At the end of every term, I would tidy all my papers, record the learning points, and just stop." He beamed at me. "It was amazing how fresh I was after every vacation." His smile faded as he realized the implications.

"Salim, if you were more at ease with all four seasons of the cycle, do you feel you'd be more at ease with your work overall? Would it help your stress level?"

He stared at me, almost fiercely. I imagined his logic circuits glowing pink as he tried to get past the limitations of the left brain.

"Well, hypothetically, yes. But empirically, the facts are against it. I have never enjoyed these spring and autumn seasons in my work. How could it ever be different?"

Balancing the cycles

"Salim, if you want to balance the cycle, it's perfectly doable," I said. "You've got the intelligence to achieve it. With this medical, you've got the motivation. And I can offer you the methods."

He was frowning anxiously. "I'm not convinced, Alan. But let's try it."

"OK. You remember we talked about energy cycles in the last workshop? If there's a blockage at any point in the cycle, the flow is impeded, right?"

Salim gave a strange, tense smile. "My God, this is just like my arteries. When the flow is blocked, the pressure rises. Go on."

"So one benefit of tracing the flow through the cycle is to see where the blockages are. Then we can apply a composting process to them."

Salim shook his head. "How do you mean?"

I went on. "Take your resistance to starting and seeding projects. Instead of denying it, magnify it, go right into it, then you can change it. My guess, Salim, is that your block about the spring season is partly because your standing in other people's eyes matters so much to you."

Salim sat up. "Of course it matters."

"Yes, but I'd say you care too much about their opinion of you. And you think it depends on you getting everything right, so you avoid giving commitments. You're afraid of failing, so you don't want to start."

He leaned forward, staring at me. "But there's no other way, is there? Since I was a young lad, always the same: good work, good boy; bad work, bad boy."

I met his glance, choosing my words carefully. "I can see it's a deeply held belief for you, but I'd call it baggage—unhelpful baggage. You're carrying it around and it's dragging you back. I mean, you talked about empirical data, Salim. Do you really believe you have to get everything right?"

He was wriggling in his chair. "Yes, I have to get it right. No, it's... I don't know..."

"Why don't we check it out?" I asked. "Why don't we go and ask Aziz?"

In Aziz's office, I explained the situation and simply asked him, "Can you tell us what you most value about Salim?"

Aziz answered readily. "Salim, what I value most about you is your technical genius. I can tell you honestly, I wouldn't sleep so well at night without you here. I just feel that whatever crises we have on the software, you can solve."

Salim frowned at him. "So my value to Virosoft depends on getting things right every time."

Aziz looked at him with surprise. "No. And that isn't what I said, Salim." He laughed. "My God, if that was true, you'd have lasted as long as a snowball in August. I mean, do you remember Maxim 2? You were five months behind your completion date, and when you'd signed it off, we still had problems, remember?"

Salim wiped his forehead. "I hate signoffs, in the end I just close my eyes and jump."

Aziz smiled warmly at him. "Yes, but I still love you Salim. You are a technical genius, but that doesn't mean you have to be perfect. You're allowed to make mistakes sometimes."

"Did you hear that, Salim?" I asked.

I could see him relaxing. "Yes," he said, "I'm allowed to make mistakes."

The monotony of challenges

"Aziz, there's a second question I'd like to ask you," I said. "Salim and I have been looking at his workload. It's depleting him because it's become monotonous."

Aziz looked startled. "Monotonous? You know, I find that quite insulting. We have an exciting business, growing fast, full of challenges..."

Salim interrupted. "Aziz, that's the problem. It's all challenges. I spend my whole time firefighting."

I added, "I'm sure you'd get more out of Salim if his work were cyclical."

Aziz was irritated. "You know, I'm really not following this conversation. What do you mean, cyclical?"

"Like growing crops in the field," I said. "To sustain the output, you need a rotation cycle. The high-output crop is followed by a renewal crop, which restores the fertility."

Aziz was getting fidgety. "I don't think I have the time for all this. What bothers me is getting Maxim 3 developed. How does this help?"

"Let's go back, then," I said. "You said, Aziz, that what you most valued in Salim was his technical genius. So your main need is for him and his team to resolve your technical problems. Is that right?"

Aziz nodded. "Absolutely."

I turned to Salim. "And that work is pretty demanding for you, isn't it?"

Salim nodded. "Draining. It's not just technical, it's the people. That's what takes it out of me."

"OK. So if that takes it out of you," I asked him, "what would put it back? Aziz really needs you to do this work. What would renew you?"

Aziz was at last getting it. "Come on Salim, just say what you need. We want to sustain you."

Salim looked anguished, like a young boy afraid to ask for what he wants.

"Remember Brunel," I said. "What worked for you there?"

Suddenly he relaxed and smiled. "OK, I'll tell you what would renew me, what would actually keep me going. One thing is being free to do my own research. Not here, but on my own, no interruptions, one or two days a week. I get so much energy from creative time like that... And the other thing is holidays. I'd say I..."

"But you take your four weeks, don't you?" Aziz asked.

Salim looked keenly back at him. "Do you realize I work a 70-hour week, including all the time at home? You're not getting the best from me, Aziz, far from it. I really need several weeks a year when I stop completely, no thinking, no work, just lying fallow."

I stepped in. "The suggestion I'd like to make to you both is that you appoint a technical operations manager under Salim. Someone who handles the project management and the personnel issues. That way, Salim would only be firefighting where he's really needed, and he'd have time for the renewal part of the cycle."

The appointment was made within a few weeks. Salim's health and productivity improved immediately. He started to initiate ideas, not just react to requests. He even took up ten-pin bowling with his team every Tuesday night. He told me, "I'm relaxed enough to talk with them, now I don't have to manage everything. And we get a lot of problems solved, just unwinding together." However, it still took some time for Salim to become less of a perfectionist and to learn to work cyclically.

"You won't be able to please everyone all the time," I told him. "Sometimes you'll have people hammering at you and you'll just have to say no. Ask them to talk to Lorna, your new operations manager. Or just don't be here."

He stared at me. "How can I not be here?"

"Lots of ways, Salim," I answered. "And if you're going to stay sane and cyclical, you'll probably have to stay out of this office a couple of days a week. As you said, it's quiet time on your own that renews you. Work at home. Have a second office, hidden in the warehouse. Put your phone on voicemail. You have to create the cycles: if you go with the pressures of the job, they'll exhaust you again."

The Cultivation Cycle: The Four Seasons

The cultivation cycle is the basis of production on any farm, although it is used more fully in organic systems. The cycle of the seasons may seem obvious to you. Yet Salim Hussain's experience of it is typical of many I have seen. Perhaps because the cycle is simple and familiar, applying it to our work can yield surprisingly powerful insights.

This cycle in the work context is summarized in Figure 9. As you look at this, consider some of the questions I asked Salim Hussain and explore them for your own work. In your working cycle, are some seasons exaggerated and others avoided? Do some tasks in each season get fully addressed, while others are skimped? With forced methods, parts of the cycle can be

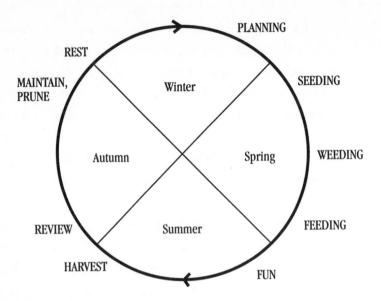

Figure 9 Cultivation cycle: the four seasons

overridden or short-circuited for some time before the problems become severe or apparent. But for sustainable natural production, all stages of the cycle are required.

Although the four seasons in farming relate to an annual cycle, in your work you need to move through these seasons more often. To some extent, you need them all daily, weekly, and monthly. They should also be reflected in the cycle of project or team activities.

Even on the organic farm, each of the seasons isn't exactly three months long and activities don't always align with the cycle of the calendar year. For instance, some crops are sown in autumn and harvested in spring. In the human work context, there will typically be a number of tasks at different stages of this cycle.

The four seasons model might imply that each season should be of equal length, but for the workplace this is hardly realistic or appropriate and the autumn and winter phases are likely to be squeezed. While the activities of these two seasons can be done in quite a short period, one of the crucial aspects of these more receptive seasons is open space time, when a deeper understanding can emerge as the groundwork and seed for the next turn of the cycle. Recognize which seasons you and an organization over- and underemphasize—contrasts between the two can be illuminating.

Winter preparation

In the cultivation cycle, each season is a prelude to the next. The winter period of rest and review creates the platform for spring growth. The cold weather means that biological activity in the soil is largely dormant; this rest helps build the energy reserves for the intense growth ahead. Freezing and thawing open up soil structures, doing the groundwork for the spring. This is also the time when the farmer reviews ground condition and output needs, and plans the spring plantings. Winter is a time for slower processes, such as preparation and integration. Manure applied in the autumn is slowly mixing into the soil, enriching the humus.

In terms of human work, this is the season for rest, renewal, and groundwork. Even a short downtime—a pause for stillness, reflection, and perspective—can be helpful. It's a stage in the cycle where you should review and renew your ground condition: improving structure, mixing in compost, so that you are ready for the coming growth. This is also a time for groundwork in the sense of planning your crop, looking ahead through the whole cycle to prepare for it: making a schedule, identifying skills or resources you need.

Spring: the delicate start

Seeding and establishing the crop is a time of intense human activity. Getting the growth process started is the most delicate and crucial stage in the cycle. The soil may need final preparation for planting. Perhaps plowing, to aerate, stimulate fertility, and improve the structure. Perhaps harrowing, where metal spikes are drawn across the surface of the field to kill weeds and break down lumps of soil. Or sometimes rolling, to create a finer, smoother topsoil.

Planting the seed is a vulnerable stage. It offers useful parallels with starting work projects, especially if we look at planting in the market garden rather than field-scale crops. Ground condition and planting methods have a significant influence on the success rate of the crop. If the soil is too cold or too dry, the seed will not germinate: the process of growth won't even begin. If the ground is too wet, the seed will rot instead of grow. Some plants will be started indoors, in protected conditions; these seedlings must be hardened off, acclimatized, before they are exposed to outdoor conditions. In this early phase, the plants are vulnerable to weather extremes, such as heavy frost, rain, or drought. Close attention, forethought, and quick response can bring the young crop through such problems: for example applying a mulch, a layer of straw, helps to protect it.

The right conditions for seeding and growing the desired plants will also stimulate the weeds. Slow-growing crops, which need time to get established, are especially at risk of being out-competed for resources by weeds, which are often vigorous and fast-growing. Hence this period of early growth is the busiest time for weed control. For some crops, spring will be a time for feeding as well as seeding and weeding. Fast-growing, nutrient-hungry crops such as tomatoes may need supplementary help.

Does this have parallels for your work? Creating a new product, starting a new task, is more like cultivating a plant than turning on a computer. Your success rate and speed of growth will be helped by freeing up time to give plentiful attention to this season: preparing the ground, providing a balanced supply of the four growth elements, protecting the new crop, and dealing with weeds and weather problems as they arise. Watering is especially important—nourishing the new starts with love and appreciation. Bear in mind that problems are likely to grow fast, as weeds do, and draw on the tools of co-creativity to handle them. And recognize that this season demands a lot of resources, so ease up on other demands on your energy and line up as much support for yourself as you can.

Summer: letting it roll

It took several years for me to get used to the ease-up phase on the farm in early summer. At first it seemed strange that the most intense plant growth is a time of lower human activity. Around late May and June, if the establishment work has gone well, the organic farmer can to some extent sit back and enjoy watching the plants grow. It is in fact a good example of co-creativity: the active phase in spring cycles into a more receptive time in early summer, which cycles into the active period in mid and late summer as harvesting begins.

In contrast, one of the risks of the mechanistic approach to work is trying too hard. Having geared ourselves up for intense effort, we keep going until we are exhausted and don't know when to stop. One lesson of the summer season is to know when to stop pushing and allow natural growth to take over. It is quite possible to have recreation and celebration at the height of the growth process, not just at the end.

During summer, most crops should be growing strongly and rapidly, approaching fruition. This is a good example of how fast natural productivity can be if the right conditions are created. However, for some crops further management may be needed: hoeing out weeds or thinning the crop so that the strongest plants can reach their full potential. In the workplace you don't have to make natural growth happen, but you may need to steer it. And sometimes the number of growth projects has to be thinned down, to achieve full maturity.

Autumn: the harvest

Harvesting, gathering in the completed crop, lasts through summer into autumn. It is a good reminder for our work that harvest time is an extended period. There may be several stages in moving from the field crop to the finished product. Consider wheat: once the plant is cut, the grain must be separated from the husk and the stalk. It then has to be dried before being further processed. Similarly, in your work allow time to harvest the full value and nutrition from your outputs.

Autumn brings us to completion of the gathering-in phase and the time of harvest festival. Appreciating and celebrating the fruits of the earth and our labor is another basic element in the sustainable cycle. Then, as plant growth slows right down, we move into the autumn activities of pruning, maintenance, and gathering our stores: preparing for winter. On the farm or market garden, there is considerable work to do at this stage to complete the year's cycle but the pace can be slower. For example, fruit and root vegetables may need to be packed and stored so that they are available in the winter. It is also a time for pruning, cutting back old growth to improve the coming year's production. And it is a time for checking ground condition at the end of the output phase, to see what maintenance and renewal are required.

In the workplace, the autumn season is vital in making the growth cycle sustainable as well as productive. This is the time for reviewing and learning, tending and regenerating your production capacity. This is also where you get the full fruits of your crop: through learning, celebration, and knowing how to process and store some of the output. Without this, you risk getting only superficial satisfaction from the whole growth cycle.

Aligning with the seasons

Think about the times when the content of your work has been in line with the season of the year. Did this make the work easier? For example, I scheduled the main period of writing this book from May through September, which helped me to be aligned with the months of full growth in the natural world. By October and November, it was harder to keep my output going.

If you can align your work tasks with the seasons, it can boost your effectiveness. Clearly this is often impossible, in which case make allowances, compensating as best you can. If I know I have a high-output project in the winter, I will schedule some rest time before and after and minimize other demands on my time. If I need to do review and maintenance in the summer, I will look for a smaller project where I can enjoy seasonal growth.

The Cultivation Cycle Checklist is a simple tool for assessing yourself, a team, or an organization for balance and completeness in the cultivation cycle. Give each item a rating from 0—total neglect, through 5—balance, to 10—major overemphasis.

CYCLE STAGE	YOUR RATING
Ground preparation: planning, nurturing the starting phase	
Seeding: using creativity	
Weeding: learning through problems, maintaining clarity	
Feeding: raising momentum by support, vision, and appreciation	
Fun: enjoying, celebrating, enabling enthusiasm to produce results	
Harvesting: bringing projects to completion, reaping full benefit for the organization and individuals	
Review: drawing out the learning and appreciating people	
Maintaining: preparing/renewing/pruning for future growth	
Rest: yes, rest!	

The competence cycle

The four seasons cycle can also be seen as a model of any learning or change process. To explore this I developed the competence cycle model with one of my colleagues, Barry Seward-Thompson, combining the seasons cycle with his work on learning competences. It is summarized in Figure 10.

While this model can be applied in many ways, one of the most revealing concerns a person's overall relationship to their job. Some people move through their job cycle too quickly, jumping to another position during the summer phase before they or the organization have reaped the full harvest of their potential. Others stay too long, often stagnating in the winter phase for years.

It is easy to overlook your own shift from high to low competence on this cycle. If your job is repetitious, you may get used to a low level of energy and achievement. Moving yourself from the winter phase and starting the cycle again need not mean changing jobs: sometimes you can reconfigure the job or set yourself new learning goals within it.

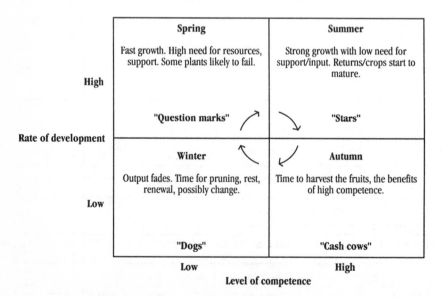

Figure 10 Competence cycle

If we consider this as a model of learning and change situations generally, what the cyclical principle emphasizes is balance and completeness: moving through each stage of the cycle, giving full attention to each in turn, finding an appropriate speed, keeping moving without rushing or stalling.

Renewal Rotation

The basic principle of crop rotation cycles is to grow a variety of crops on each piece of land. It contrasts with the mono-culture on conventional farms, where the same crop is grown on the same land for several years. One of the key organic crop rotations is a cycle alternating between a high-value, demanding crop like wheat, and a fertility-building crop such as clover. This cycle takes many forms, some quite sophisticated with eight or ten "courses," and the complete cycle could take as much as ten years. Besides renewing fertility, crop rotation also achieves pest and weed prevention by natural means.

This use of rotation is an example of increasing the level of change and variation to reduce problems. It echoes a theme in *Blur*, a book by Davis and Meyer on managing change: they believe that the best way to handle rising speed and complexity is often to increase them further.

Renewal rotation at work

The equivalent to crop rotation in your work could be rotation between tasks, between jobs, or between different modes of working. The potential benefits for your personal ecosystem are similar to those of the organic farm. Rotation between tasks is probably the simplest approach, although rotation between jobs works superbly for some people.

The third option, varying your mode of working, is in some ways the easiest but requires more self-discipline. It depends on your own awareness to make the change and alter your habits. A simple way to do this is to notice your customary ways of working and thinking, and periodically choose the less habitual ones. For example, if you mostly react to problems in a left-brain, analytical mode, try easing off, freewheeling, going for a short walk, making space for your right brain to contribute.

The primary criteria in creating rotation cycles in your work should be balance and renewal and the avoidance of mono-culture or excessive repetition. Observe what you overdo and create cycles to counterbalance this. There are several frame-works you can use for this investigation. One is the principle of sustaining ground condition and its link to personal energy. If you regularly drive yourself too hard and make too many demands on your fertility, clearly you need more renewal activities. Conversely, if you are understretched in your work, you may need to add more challenging crops to that cycle and raise your vitality. You could achieve this through a range of unpaid work and leisure activities.

The Eight Rhythms Checklist opposite can be used to explore this. Considering your usual working style, for each pair of qualities score yourself from 0—I don't do this at all, to 10—major overemphasis. You can add your own ideas on the blank lines.

Designing your cycle

Designing a rotation cycle is a co-creative process. You can ana-lyze some factors, such as soil type, climate conditions, current market demand, and your own capabilities and goals. But intu-ition is needed to guess at the uncertainties, anticipate future customer needs, and adjust to surprises as the rotation pro-gresses. There are some specific methods used in rotation that offer ideas for human activity cycles at work.

The Eight Rhythms checklist

	10	8	5	3	0	0	3	5	8	10	
Active	—	—	—	—	—	—	—	—	—	—	Reflective
Production	—	—	—	—	—	—	—	—	—	—	Maintenance
Preparation	—	—	—	—	—	—	—	—	—	—	Implementation
Broad exploration	—	—	—	—	—	—	—	—	—	—	Focused action
Change/risk	—	—	—	—	—	—	—	—	—	—	Stability/safety
Independent	—	—	—	—	—	—	—	—	—	—	Collaborative
Stretching	—	—	—	—	—	—	—	—	—	—	Renewing
Playful	—	—	—	—	—	—	—	—	—	—	Serious
....	—	—	—	—	—	—	—	—	—	—	....
....	—	—	—	—	—	—	—	—	—	—	....

Intercropping

This method, also known as polyculture, involves growing two crops on the same land at the same time. Although it can make cultivation and harvesting more difficult, it has several benefits. Typically the overall productive yield is greater. The growth potential of the four elements is used more fully and efficiently and there is literally less space for weeds to develop. Particular combinations of plants can be specially synergistic and prevent pest problems. For example, if onions and carrots are intercropped, the onions repel the carrot flies.

The inference for the workplace is that combining activities can be mutually reinforcing and raise your energy productivity. An example is Salim Hussain, intercropping research and lecturing. If one of your main activities draws heavily on certain talents, choosing a complementary task alongside it can be the best way to achieve balance. I have seen a computer programmer take up massage part-time and a management trainer branch into landscape gardening. This is different from renewal rotation because you can sometimes produce two demanding crops together if they are synergistic.

Green manures

This refers to crops grown in order to raise fertility: typically, the entire crop is plowed back into the earth as a form of compost. In medieval times, fields were left completely fallow and dormant for one year in three to restore them. Nowadays, a fertility-building crop or a green manure would be preferred. A vigorous fast-growing green manure can reduce weed problems by beating them in the competition for growth resources.

The concept of green manures highlights how maximizing output value doesn't happen by an exclusive focus on growing the target crop. Other approaches, including rest and fertility building, also need to be included. Teambuilding and other development processes are examples of green manures for an organization. The business simulation we ran for Alibi Publishing certainly worked in this way.

Trap crops

One of the artful ways in which organic farmers reduce pests is to start growing a crop to attract them and then to plow the crop in, killing the pests at the same time. The use of trap crops gives another example of intensifying a problem in order to resolve it.

I have used this method to good effect when initiating a new project or a new team. Getting them working on a difficult and even provocative dummy project for a day or two brought more of the problems to the surface, so we could debug them before getting on with the main work.

Undersowing

This is the principle of sowing the seed for the next crop before the preceding one is fully grown and harvested. In most situations an organic farmer will avoid leaving the earth uncovered, i.e. without a crop of some kind. Bare, unused earth is more prone to weeds and to soil erosion. Undersowing maintains continuity of cover and uses the earth productively, as one crop begins before the other is finished. The first crop is usually harvested while the seeds of the new one are germinating underground.

At work, this approach can have the benefits of continuity and extra gestation time. Approaching the completion of a project can be a bumpy period, as people speculate about what's coming next. If the seeds of the next project are sown before the harvest of the last one, it gives more time for creativity to germinate and for new working relationships to put down roots before high output is required.

Catch crops

Catch crops are grown opportunistically, during the gap between major crops with longer growth cycles. The crop might be a green manure or an output crop with a short growth cycle.

This method offers a way for an individual or a team to bring more renewal into the cycle. Even a short task can rebuild fertility or give a sense of a quick win between longer, more complex projects.

Bastard fallow

This is another ingenious method of intensifying the growth of weeds in order to eliminate them. It means leaving a field without a crop, usually just for a few weeks. Various methods may be used to stimulate maximum weed growth during this period, for example creating a false seed bed, which is prepared and cultivated as if for an output crop but no crop is sown. The weed seeds are thus given maximum encouragement to germinate. As the weed plants grow, they can be plowed under as compost.

In the work context, this is probably a high-risk strategy! I would only follow it if I felt there was a severe problem with weeds: dissatisfaction, buried conflicts, energy leaks. An example would be a department left temporarily without a boss. If there are difficulties this is one way to flush them out; however, it needs to be structured in order to face the problems constructively. A mild example is the workshop we ran for Alibi Publishing without the dominant presence of Phil Morris. His subordinates were not used to resolving their issues directly with each other, but by providing both skills and a safe context they were able to do so.

The Nutrient Cycle

Cultivating natural systems is a matter of knowing when and how to intervene, to harness a natural process with minimum human effort. While a conventional farm depends heavily on importing synthetic nutrients, the organic farm generates its own and operates both horizontal and vertical nutrient cycles to move them to where they are needed.

Some fertility is produced where it is required, such as growing clover or green manure on a particular field. It is also valuable to have a source of discretionary fertility, which can be moved to where you want it, known as horizontally cycling nutrients. For many organic farms, this comes from the winter housing of cattle. While the cows are kept under cover for the winter, their dung mixes with the bedding straw, composting to create manure. This can then be shifted to where it is most needed, typically fields being prepared for high-value crops like cereals.

The implication for the workplace is to be aware of where you can generate compost and how to shift it to meet your main energy demands. The horizontal cycle means gathering positive energy from one aspect of your life and work and applying it to the current need. For example, a sense of appreciation may be an important motivator to you and may be missing in a current project. If so, harness it elsewhere and carry that feeling into this project.

Vertical cycling means moving nutrients within the soil. When rainwater passes through topsoil it carries nutrients down into the subsoil, beyond the reach of many plants. A crop rotation should therefore include some deep-rooting crops that will reach into the subsoil and draw nutrients back up. For example, the roots of red clover or field lupins can go as deep as five or six feet.

People talk of digging deep into their reserves, implying that they are close to exhausted. The analogy with ground condition suggests that if you dig deep, or better still grow deep, there will be more nutrients available to you. Vertical cycling in your work means drawing such nutrients from deeper in your ground condition: from past experience or from your subconscious.

Harnessing subconscious resources is hard to do directly: it is more a co-creative process, where you consciously identify the need, but leave the right brain, intuition, to get on with the work for you. There are some processes that can help this, equivalent to the deep-rooting plants used for vertical nutrient cycling on the farm. Kalita Homelux illustrates how the nutrients deep within the human condition can be brought to the topsoil.

Kalita Homelux

The scene was an anonymous hotel in Belgium. I was leading a workshop for the sales managers of this major European manufacturer of domestic appliances. It was a change management workshop, using The Natural Advantage, and the main aim was to help the sales management team adapt constructively to a forthcoming reorganization. But there was a secondary agenda:

this was mid-December and it was also the team's Christmas get-together, so I couldn't get too earnest with them.

The team had a pretty successful track record, but their confidence had drained away during this year when their sales performance had been below target, one of the reasons for the reorganization. Their ground condition was depleted and I knew that this next round of changes was making them edgy: vertical nutrient cycling was one of my objectives for the session. Just as a hard rain carries nutrients down into the subsoil, the recent outbursts of criticism and insecurity had washed nutrients out of their topsoil.

I explained to the team that I would like them to explore how they had managed change in the past, to help them develop ways to meet it in the future. I put them in pairs to review the changes they had handled in the past ten years. To add some fun and to widen the perspective, I asked half of them to be themselves and gave different roles to the others. One of these was Jean-Claude, a Frenchman in his fifties who was known to be anti-German and anti-feminist. I gave him the role of Fraulein Grunkopf, the head of the German Green Party. Another was Andrea di Grasso, probably the most arrogant and ambitious member of the sales team. I asked her to play the role of Lars Blom, their chief executive. Twists like this got them laughing and unwinding, so that they could be more freely creative.

As I had suspected, they loved reminiscing about the good old days, how simple, slow, and easy things had been. It also drew out their appreciation of the scale of change, and the way they kept meeting challenges that seemed impossible at the time. In effect, this was drawing nutrients up from their subsoil, from their memory, their subconscious—cycling them into the topsoil where they could be harnessed.

When I asked them to picture the future, they were able to voice their fears, exaggerate them, and laugh about them.

Andrea's picture was "In ten years' time, we have only one employee left in Europe. The good news is it's me, Lars. The bad news is, I work for the computer." By freeing up their tensions, and drawing on the nutrients of past success, they moved on to a view of the future that was both realistic and optimistic.

Cycles in the Organization

Most organizations are still very far from acknowledging or developing human sustainability: their prevailing culture and practices do not sit easily with natural cycles. Typically, the word "cycle" would only be used to describe the planning or budgeting procedure.

Despite this, a growing number of companies now acknowledge pressures pulling them toward natural systems approaches. These issues include dissatisfaction with work–life balance among many workers at all levels and ages; the reluctance of a rising number of graduates to consider a business career because they dislike the pressures; and the continuing increase in stress-related problems. Recent compensation awards in the courts show that employers are increasingly being held responsible for stress and depletion in their staff. And some trends in the workplace are encouraging—flexitime, home working, and the virtual office all offer potential for working cyclically.

The real motivation to address these issues comes when there is a business benefit as well as a human one. Improving the quality of working life can be acknowledged as desirable, but won't of itself get the issue on to a company's action agenda. To align its culture with natural cycles, an organization or team should start with the business's needs and results. If the culture can promote the idea that full and balanced cycles are good for the business, then cycles are likely to take root. If using both sides of the brain, slowing down to harvest, rest and review, and rotating high output with renewal tasks are endorsed as helpful to the profits as well as the people, this will create the ground conditions from which appropriate skills and processes can develop.

Examples do exist of businesses that have improved performance by humanizing their culture, some of which are described in *The Dance of Change*. The Japanese business culture particularly endorses cyclical approaches. *The Art of Japanese Management* by Pascale and Athos compares Japanese and American large businesses. They comment that in a Japanese office, sitting at your desk staring meditatively into space would be regarded as acceptable and in fact productive behavior. In an American business you'd probably be bawled out within a minute.

Cyclical work processes can include such approaches as job enrichment, where members of a team learn additional skills so that each person performs a range of tasks. There is also job rotation, where individuals move between jobs more frequently. In Japan this is called the spiral staircase model of career progression. Instead of climbing vertically up the hierarchy within one department, people move more slowly, diagonally upward, through a series of different job functions. This philosophy is coming into favor in western businesses following the trend to flatter organizational structures.

Processes can also be used to encourage the full four seasons cycle and the balance of left- and right-brain thinking. Established methods often focus on one or two seasons of the cycle and on one way of thinking, usually the active, analytical approach. The story of David Marsing at Intel, quoted in Chapter 6, is a good example of using a meeting cycle to create a balanced approach, by encouraging receptive peripheral vision.

A further example from *The Dance of Change* of using a process to create cyclicality involves Lotte Bailyn, of MIT Sloan School of Management:

"Sometimes a different way of structuring time can make a difference. We conducted a time experiment with one product development team who worked excessively long hours. We originally proposed closing the doors at 6pm and making everybody leave, but they wouldn't hear of it. They knew that this wouldn't get to the core of their problem. Individuals couldn't finish their work because they were constantly interrupted by meetings, schedule checks, and management reviews.

"We worked with them to restructure the workday into 'quiet times' and 'interactive times.' The results were astounding: the team launched the product on time and received quality rewards. Moreover, they now felt a greater sense of control, which eased some of their personal stress. The managers learned that engineers perform better without continuous surveillance. The VP even gave up his weekly ops reviews."

Both culture and processes are important in helping organizations and their people manage the competence cycle to best effect. Better processes, such as succession planning and human development reviews, are one way to manage this cycle better. However, the speed of change makes such anticipation difficult.

An alternative is the approach used by a major British telecommunications equipment manufacturer for its professional engineers. The company recognized that most people no longer expect a job for life and are skeptical about an employer's ability to plan their career for them. It ran career-management workshops for its engineers. By giving them the skills to clarify their personal goals, handle career uncertainties, and assert what they want from the company, it has empowered each individual to manage their competence cycle. This organization believes that if the individuals are motivated and in appropriate positions, this will achieve the best productive results for the business.

Cycles in Daily Practice

As you start to change your habits and seek a counterbalance to some of the pressures on you, formal methods can be useful. Scheduling quiet time in your diary will help you keep your commitments to balancing the cycle, as it did in Lotte Bailyn's work with the product development team. In the early stages of the transition, reviewing your ways of working every week or month will ensure that you regularly check which parts of the cycle are neglected and where you need to balance your approach. Over time, you should find that you start to balance your activities and operate with cycles instinctively and habitually.

8
Resilience Through Diversity

If you clear a piece of land and leave it be, over many years its ecosystem will become increasingly sophisticated and sustainable. Initially, it will be a crude or pioneer ecosystem with a small number of species and little diversity. The pioneer species, many of them weeds, consume fertility, grow fast, but produce low-quality outputs. Over time more diverse, slow-growing species will take over. This process culminates in what are called climax ecosystems, of which rainforests are a classic example. These are highly diverse, self-sustaining, and produce an abundance of crops and fruits useful to humans and other creatures.

If you look at the overall human use of environmental resources, what kind of ecosystem does it equate to? Despite recent progress, it's more like a pioneer than a climax system. The same is true of human energy resources at work, so the potential for improvement is great. Diversity plays an important role in this evolution, and organic farms offer particularly useful examples. They make constructive use of biodiversity, but also embody customer and enterprise diversity. Whether you work full time for one organization or freelance for many, you can increase the diversity in your ways of working.

Alison's Redundancy

Out of the blue I received a phone call from Alison Martin, the middle manager with the National Health Service whose story is featured in Chapters 2 and 4. She was distraught. "Alan, they've made me redundant from the NHS. I'm at my wit's end, honestly. Can I meet you to talk about it?"

A few days later, we converged on Magdalen Farm. It was a blustery March afternoon when showers and sunny spells alternated rapidly. Alison glared at me when we met.

"You seem angry," I began.

"Angry!" She burst out. "I'm sodding furious if you really want to know."

"At?" I asked.

Alison scowled, but her hunched shoulders straightened up as she described her feelings. "At you. At me. At them. Everything I depended on has let me down. I mean, I really trusted you."

"But I couldn't save you from this, could I?" I asked gently.

Alison shook her head, and moved from anger to tears. "It was going so well. I was actually enjoying the bloody job for the first time in years, and then... It's like being thrown out of a plane without a parachute."

Later, after a cup of tea, we strolled through the fields beside the River Axe. "So where do I go from here?" Alison asked.

I looked at her. "Well, let's take stock for a minute. How is your ground condition?"

She blew her nose. "A bit waterlogged right now, but basically pretty good. I feel I manage my energy pretty well most of the time." Alison grinned at me. "And you don't have to remind me about composting all this anger and fear. I will do it, you know."

"So if we stay with the farming analogy," I said, "what is this redundancy like?"

There was a long pause as we walked on. At last she said, "It's like a crop failure, on a giant scale. It feels like my entire farm has been wiped out by one freak event."

"Go on. Where in farming do you see that kind of problem?"

There was another long pause. "Ah yes!" she suddenly exclaimed. "It's like those resistant strains that Peter talks about. On conventional farms, you get superpests evolving that are immune to the chemicals, the pesticides."

I smiled to myself. This was starting to get somewhere. "But how," I asked innocently, "would one pest wipe out an entire farm?"

"It's obvious," she said. "It's that monoculture thing you talk about. Very common with intensive farms, right? The whole farm put down to one crop. The more years you go on with that one crop, the more vulnerable you are, and the more dependent..." Her voice tailed off as the penny dropped. She laughed and punched me on the arm. "OK, smartass, I get the message! You walked me neatly into that one. And you're right. Even though the Health Service has changed like crazy, I kept my job largely the same. For the last 12 years I've been a medical records manager."

"So you thought if you were indispensable, you were safe?" I asked.

Alison nodded, "Exactly. I've gone stale in the job, but it was my way of limiting change to what I thought I could cope with. Anyhow, I get the point. You can impose monoculture for so long, then the problems burst out, mega style. What do I do about it?"

I smiled. "Sounds like time to go and ask Christopher Robin."

We found Peter Norman in the polytunnel, a form of greenhouse made of polythene sheet over arched metal frames.

Alison stared around her. "What kind of things have you planted here?"

"A lot of different varieties," Peter answered. "Let's see... tomatoes, three kinds. Lettuces, five kinds. Pak choi, salad herbs, three types of cucumber..."

"It sounds horribly complicated," Alison exclaimed. "Can't you make it simpler for yourselves?"

Peter laughed. "We'd rather not, leastways not yet. We've planted a lot of different things to see what likes it here."

Alison snorted. "That's ridiculous! Surely you can look that stuff up in a book?"

He looked surprised. "Not really. Every piece of land is unique: the soil type, pests, predators, diseases, history, it's all a unique combination. By planting five kinds of lettuce, I've a good chance of finding a couple of winners. If I planted one or two, I might get an OK one and I might have complete failure."

"But once you've got a winner, you'll stick with it?" Alison persisted.

Peter frowned. "Not so simple. The longer I repeat the same crop in the same place, the more I risk problems. After three years, I'd either change the crop or move the whole polytunnel to a fresh piece of soil."

Alison looked around the polytunnel dubiously. "I still don't get it, Peter. In my mother's greenhouse, she's always spraying like crazy to keep the pests down. I mean, what you're doing here is fairly repetitious, isn't it?"

Peter gave one of his vague smiles. "Yes, it is a bit intensive, and I don't know why it works, really. It's basically a matter of trusting the system."

Alison growled. "How the hell am I supposed to learn from an answer like that?"

"What I mean," Peter answered, "is that if the general system is right you don't have to take specific actions to prevent pests. The field margins are pretty crucial, but I couldn't say exactly how."

"What do you mean, field margins?"

"Most organic farmers leave an uncultivated margin round the edge of their fields," Peter explained. "That provides a space for wild flowers, wild grasses, and weeds. The field margins provide a habitat for birds and insects, like the hedges do. It means that whatever pests we have, we've usually got the predators around too. So most of the time, nature keeps things in balance for us."

"Don't you ever get major disasters?" Alison asked. "You know, a whole crop wiped out at a stroke, so it brings you to your knees?"

Peter shook his head. "Very rarely. Sometimes we get crops and livestock below the target yield, or running late, but I'll still earn something on it. And anyway, it's only one string to my guitar."

"Can you explain the guitar?" I asked.

Peter smiled. "I say that a monoculture farm is like a guitar with one string. It's horribly boring for everyone, and if your one string breaks you really are screwed. Magdalen Farm is like an eight-string guitar. If one of them breaks, I can busk it for a while. All the strings resonate and enrich the music. That way, you get this synergy that Alan's always on about."

The Jelly of Biodiversity

Understanding and applying the principle of biodiversity is as difficult as nailing jelly to a wall, but infinitely more useful. As Stephen Martin of The Natural Step UK says, "The current losses of biodiversity are like losing rivets on an airplane. You can lose quite a few and the plane keeps flying. If you keep losing more and more rivets, you know that at some point the plane will crash, but that point is unforecastable."

In considering why biodiversity is important, a specific example may help: human food. It is estimated that 90 percent of all human food consumption now depends on 20 plant species: rice, wheat, and potatoes being the most important of these. Within these species, the rapid growth of intensive farming worldwide means that much of this production depends on a very small number of specific plant strains, which have been specially bred for high yields under intensive conditions. This has already produced several major crises. For example, in 1993 80 percent of the North American maize crop was under threat of destruction by a single disease. The risk was only averted because the maize strain was enhanced by crossing it with a much older strain from Mexico.

Because of the extremely high use of a single strain of species such as wheat, these strains have to be replaced or enhanced every 10–15 years. The source of the improvement is usually an obscure, traditional strain. If we turn to the analogy with the workplace, how many species of working style and culture account for those in most large organizations? As with intensive farming, the pressures for immediate output have led to a steep increase in conformity.

The rise of intensive farming is a significant cause of lost biodiversity. The dramatic increase in pesticide use since the 1950s has killed off numerous insect species. Many of these insects brought benefits as well as problems: for example providing food for the birds who kept slug levels in check. The push to maximize production led many intensive farms to eliminate hedgerows and other habitats, which had supported a large variety of plants and wildlife.

Diversity on the farm

Any farm is less biodiverse than nature in the wild, but the organic farmer actively fosters diversity. As Peter's polytunnel illustrates, this is achieved by cultivating a wider range of crops and livestock, often choosing plant species and animal breeds that are more traditional and less common. The seed mix for an organic pasture will typically contain 10–15 varieties of grass, clover, and herbs, while a conventional mix might simply be one strain of grass. In fact, organic standards specifically require farmers to "maintain the genetic diversity of the agricultural system and its surroundings, including the protection of plant and wildlife habitats."

Biodiversity is also helped by maintaining hedgerows, field margins, and other habitats, such as small ponds, copses, and areas of scrub. Organic farmers do this partly because it's the right thing, it's good stewardship of natural resources. They also do it because greater biodiversity adds resilience, although these benefits often can't be quantified or anticipated. Resilience is essential when you know you can't control change, since it creates the means to respond to change actively and harness it to advantage. The equivalent in human health is to develop a robust immune system, and reduce your susceptibility to the viruses and bugs to which we are all constantly exposed. The analogy to the intensive farming approach would be trying to sanitize your environment, to suppress and eliminate all the threats. This is exhausting and unsustainable.

Enterprise diversity is another aspect of the organic farm's resilience. Even a smallish holding is likely to have several business enterprises. This may mean losing some economies of scale, but it creates both internal and external resilience: if one enterprise suffers production problems, others can sustain the income flow. The enterprises will be chosen for their symbiotic benefits: the combination will be more resilient and productive than any one or two activities on their own. For example, manure from the livestock feeds the plants, and plant waste in turn is used to feed the animals. Internal resilience also rises because more diversity means more change, more rotation, and hence less risk of pests and other problems. External resilience is improved because the farm is less dependent on any one market. If demand or prices suddenly drop in one sector, this will not threaten the financial viability of the whole farm.

Enterprise diversity also makes experimentation, learning, and innovation easier—many organic farms have stumbled on a profitable market niche by accident. An intensive farm is unlikely to embark on such experiments: because labor is minimized and specialized capital equipment is used, small-scale diversification is difficult.

Livestock diversity is a feature of many organic farms. The three main types of livestock—pigs, sheep, and cattle—complement each other in the benefits they bring to ground condition: churning, conditioning, and cycling. The earth benefits from periodically being deeply churned over by pigs, who grub up persistent, deep-rooted weeds such as docks. Sheep are often called golden hoof: their light feet will aerate and condition soil that is recently sown or damp, which would be compacted by heavier animals. Cattle, as we have seen, create an excellent nutrient cycle to sustain fertility. Livestock diversity also helps to reduce pests. For example, the main sheep and cattle parasites have different lifecycles, so rotating these animals in a clean grazing system prevents both sets of parasites from building up.

The *personal diversity*, the variety of tasks and expertise needed by organic farmers and their teams, is remarkable: every organic farm is certainly a learning organization. Staff diversity is also common. Organic methods are more labor intensive: the number of hands needed has wide seasonal swings, which are met by some ingenious means. In the UK one of these is WWOOFers—Willing Workers On Organic Farms—a non-profit operation enabling people of diverse ages and backgrounds to work on organic farms, for a weekend or a few weeks, usually as volunteers receiving board and lodging. The range of people spans teenagers on probation through families to retired professionals.

Most organic farmers also have an instinctive drive toward *customer diversity*. Although big customers such as supermarkets are important to many of them, they generally seek to develop a range of customers, including some direct local links. Diversification into new products is frequently motivated by the desire to extend the customer base. This is explored further in Chapter 9.

As you consider the implications of all this for the workplace, you may conclude that an organic farm is a network of cottage industries, while an intensive farm is typical of any large-scale industrial production process, be it a factory or an office. The truth is less simple. The largest organic farms are of similar size to big factory farms: one or two thousand acres. Nevertheless, large organic farms still embody diversity, and provide a model of economic, human, and environmental sustainability that a large factory farm cannot. At this size, an organic farm will use specialized mechanical equipment and will tailor its processes to achieve economies of scale. However, it will rarely do this as a monoculture: the aim is to achieve economies of scale, but in a diversity of enterprises that provide mutual synergy.

Diversity at Work

If, like Alison Martin, you have a stretching full-time job in a large organization, the prospects of bringing diversity into your work may look poor. The pressures toward standardization and conformity can be high, and are often worse in large public-sector bodies than in business. However, there are other trends that may help you, such as flatter organizations, shifting responsibilities from service staff to line managers, matrix organization structures, and the use of project teams. These typically increase the variety and variability of individual roles, and offer more scope to harness the organization's needs to create diversity in your work content.

I have worked with many middle managers on part-time MBA programs who were doubtful if they could diversify their job within their current organization. Most were in jobs that fulfilled only a fraction of their talents and this had been a motive for doing an MBA. As their new learning showed them areas they wanted to explore in their work, their uncertainty increased. Often, the limitation was in the narrow views of their boss, or their boss's boss, not in the organization as a whole. I encouraged these managers to use their project and research work on the MBA to broaden their contacts and to discover which people, and what priorities, in their organization aligned with their diversification goals. In many cases, a fit did exist and they were able to expand or change jobs without having to change employer.

A useful method of exploring diversity in your work is Charles Handy's portfolio concept, described in his book *The Age of Unreason*. He likens the benefits of investing in a diverse portfolio of financial assets to those of investing our working energy in a range of activities. This does not necessarily mean giving up the full-time day job. As Handy says, "We will do well to broaden our definition of what work is. Instead of seeing it as paid employment, why not see it as any activity with a productive purpose?" He outlines five different types of work:

❖ *Wage work*: money paid for time worked.
❖ *Fee work*: money paid for results delivered.
❖ *Home work*: activity involved with your home and family, including cleaning, shopping, and childcare.
❖ *Gift work*: voluntary work outside the home, including work for charity or the local community.
❖ *Study work*: developing your own knowledge and skills.

Even in a demanding full-time job, you may have scope to develop two or three strands in your portfolio. Recognizing and valuing what you receive and how you can develop through work outside your main job is also important. It took me years to realize that cooking a meal for my family could be renewing.

The diversity checklist

This is designed to help you assess and cultivate diversity in your work, both at the overall, structural level and in daily practice. The first part asks you to apply Charles Handy's portfolio concept. Remember that one job position can include several roles. For example, as a department manager, your role portfolio could include: (i) the people and task responsibilities of your main work, (ii) a secondary role as mentor to several graduate trainees, (iii) membership of a creative product development project team. The work activities you list may not all be paid and may include hobbies and leisure pursuits.

1 Structural diversity

See if you can identify a portfolio of 4–8 main work activities. Number them and use these numbers for the assessment in Section 2. Tick which of Handy's categories each fits into.

	Main work activities	Wage/fee work	Home work	Gift work	Study work
1					
2					
3					
4					
5					
6					
7					
8					

If all your activities fit within one or two of these categories, check if you are defining work widely enough: it can include any activity with a productive purpose. A spread of work between at least three of these categories is desirable.

2 Client diversity

Who is/are the main client(s) for each of the 4–8 work activities you have identified above?

Client	1	2	3	4	5	6	7	8

Looking at this matrix, how do you rate the diversity of your clients/customers? (Use a scale from 0—very low, to 10—very high.)

If this diversity needs to be improved, identify three steps you can take to achieve this:

1

_____

2

_____

3

_____

3 Skill/task diversity

For each of your 4–8 work activities, identify 1–2 main skills or tasks that they involve. For example, if one activity is membership of a new product team, the main skills/tasks could be teamworking and creative development of ideas. Note on the matrix overleaf to what extent the same skills or tasks feature in several of your activities, indicating a lower level of overall diversity.

If you want to do this analysis in more detail, listing more skills/tasks for each activity, create your own matrix on a larger sheet of paper.

Looking at this matrix, how do you rate the diversity of the skills/tasks in your work as a whole? (Use a scale from 0—very low, to 10—very high.) If this diversity needs to be improved, highlight three skills or tasks that would significantly increase the diversity level:

1

_____

2

_____

3

_____

Skills/tasks	1	2	3	4	5	6	7	8

The wild margins

The tasks and skills you deliberately cultivate in your work are like the production enterprises on the organic farm. These probably take up most of the attention, most of the land area, and bring in the money. Yet we know that the fringe areas of land support a huge profusion of plant, insect, bird, and animal species. The equivalent to this in human terms may be out on the edges, the remote corners of your work. These fringes may not form part of your main, paid work. The lesson here is to value and make time for the wild margins of your nature, for those characteristics and activities that may seem marginal, frivolous or useless.

My own marginal, apparently useless passions include steam trains, Arab music, and woodworking. In my thirties I believed, rightly or wrongly, that admitting such eccentricities would damage my career and credibility in mainstream business. So I didn't disclose them, but at least I had the sense to keep doing them.

If you can identify any "wild margin" activities of your own, list them briefly below, with a couple of words on the benefits they give you. If you want to create wild margins or add more, write down your ideas on this and the benefits they might bring.

Wild margin activities	Benefits

Whatever your personal wild margins are, encourage them: they help your sustainability, even if the benefits seem intangible. We have seen how in mainstream farming, it is often obscure varieties or wild plants whose qualities are needed when an overused monoculture strain of plant hits problems. In the same way, imagine that your eccentric side could hold the key when you or your organization runs into problems and needs a creative solution.

Applying the principle

Diverse interests are sometimes best kept separate from the main job, although sometimes they can interweave to create synergy. I recall a successful sales manager for a large computer firm who still wished he had become a professional saxophone player. With a family and mortgage to support, this was not a realistic option. Bob realized that his best way through was to soundproof the garage and play around on the sax just for fun. As he said, "I don't want to make a second career of this. I have to be so disciplined and accurate in my main work, it's expressive messing about I need outside it."

By contrast, Glenda had worked in the call center of a large bank for several years. She was getting bored with it, to the point where her health and vitality were suffering. Outside the job she had developed a deep interest in tai chi, but this no longer offset the monotony and stress of her main work. In a personal development workshop I was leading, she described how bored some of her colleagues also were. One of them had jokingly said she should start a tai chi class in the lunch hour. Glenda told us this story as if it was a silly idea, but in telling it she realized its potential. Although she was nervous about leading a group, especially for colleagues, it worked. Glenda became a kind of seed bank for this group, adapting complementary methods for stress management.

Customer or client diversity is another application of the principle. This applies as much to the employed as the self-employed. If you develop your links with a range of senior contacts within the organization, you gain resilience. You and your abilities are more widely known and you gain access to a wider range of opportunities. A surprising number of people remain over-reliant on the relationship with their direct manager. This can be like monoculture: if your manager moves on, or falls out with you, you are vulnerable without a diverse customer base.

Task and skill diversity will also increase your resilience to change and help you renew your resources. Make this a criterion for the way you develop both your main work and other activities. Aim to use a wide variety of skills and develop more diverse new ones. The Eight Rhythms Checklist in Chapter 7 is one way to highlight gaps. Remember that monoculture, in this case excess repetition of one task or skill, is likely to deplete you and sap your resilience.

An example of this principle is my own career. For many years I poured most of my work energy into one job at a time. As a result, I typically exhausted my potential in that role within three or four years, and would leave to join another company. Since 1990, I have developed four strands to my work: they are diverse but mutually reinforcing. All are renewing for me and sustainable over the long term. Within my main business, Working Vision, I offer consultancy and facilitation for a variety of organizational clients. I also lead personal development workshops for individuals: these have quite a different character and enable me to experiment. My gift work since 1990 has been the establishment of the Wessex Foundation and Magdalen Farm. My main wild-margin activity has been Hazel Hill Wood, a 70-acre wood I own near Salisbury. I have indulged my love of nature, my secret desire to be an architect, and my interest in woodworking by establishing Hazel Hill as a retreat center and helping to design and construct a range of wooden buildings for this purpose. Overall, this portfolio gives me structural diversity, and also client, task, and skill diversity.

Diversity in Organizations

In her book *The Change Masters*, Rosabeth Moss Kanter explores the differences between large organizations that change successfully and those that fail. She comments that in giant groups who learn to move, the crucial expertise often comes from a subsidiary on the margins of the group. This may be seen as a maverick or rebel outfit: successful, but uncomfortably different. These wild-margin divisions may have been threatened with sell-off or cultural clampdowns in the past.

However, when the monocultural problems of the main group reach crisis level, the exiles become the new kings.

Few businesses can compete without a fair degree of focus and efficiency. The art is knowing when to draw the line: how to encourage the wild margin within the organization. A successful example of this is 3M: it requires its development engineers to spend 15 percent of their time on projects they have personally initiated, as distinct from output priorities set for the rest of their time by senior management. It was through this "wild margin" time that major new products such as Post-it Notes™ originated. 3M also has a suggestion scheme whereby any employee can request time and resources to investigate an idea for a new product or operational improvement.

Another successful approach is taken by the British non-profit organization Business in the Community, which creates opportunities for staff from large businesses to work on local social and environmental improvement projects. Typically, staff will do this during paid work time. Employers involved in the scheme, such as B&Q and Tesco, report paybacks for their businesses through the increased capabilities and motivation of the people involved.

Just as organic farmers foster biodiversity partly as a good thing in its own right, many organizations support community initiatives and other voluntary work among their staff for equally broad motives. There may be potential benefits from staff contribution to the company, or from customer attitudes, but these are too diffuse to specify. Often, the main benefit is in building resilience to change: when the company hits an unexpected problem, there are skills and support to meet it in a way that could never have been pre-planned.

The resilient patchwork

As we have seen, the diverse patchwork of crops and livestock on organic farms creates more resilience than is present in monocultures. In the same way, some leading businesses have recognized the need to increase diversity among their people. This is not specifically intended to address issues of equal opportunities and recruitment of minorities. The aim is to increase diversity along a range of criteria: thinking and learning styles, temperament, gender, age, educational level, regional and ethnic background. For example, Ann Lamont, human resources director of a BP subsidiary, comments: "To stay as successful as we have been, we know that we have to keep reinventing ourselves, thinking outside the box. We are deliberately cultivating diversity in our intake of people, to ensure that we raise the level of internal challenge, constructive conflict, so that we can change even faster than our competitive environment."

Diversity is not the same as diversification. Business diversity can be achieved in several ways. It may mean leveraging core competences through a range of different products or markets. For example, the original expertise of the Honda Corporation was motors, but it has achieved strength through diversity by applying this expertise to a variety of markets: cars, motorcycles, outboard motors, lawnmowers, generators, and others. In other cases, diversity may be achieved through a portfolio of enterprises that are basically different, but provide synergy or counterbalances.

Diversity in Daily Practice

Cycles and diversity are closely linked: they require and enable each other. If your day-to-day working style is cyclical, this will help to make it diverse. *Structural* diversity probably needs to be your main concern. If you can set up variety in your work enterprises and customer base, and if you give time to your wild margins, diversity in daily practice should flow from this.

Create new patterns to help you achieve diversity in your daily work. For example, I counter my workaholic tendency by taking regular breaks and challenging myself to do something recreational, before I go back to the main task. And remember to indulge your wild margins!

9
Real
Quality

This chapter brings us to real quality, the last of the seven principles of *The Natural Advantage*. It completes our journey through the sustainable production cycle, which started with ground condition and finishes with the quality of outputs and customer relationships. As you would expect, this last stage in the cycle feeds back into the first. If your outputs have real quality and emotional value, this naturally helps to renew your ground condition.

I use the term "real quality" to cover products and production processes that create value, including organic marketing, a range of innovative approaches to build dialogue, adaptability, and co-creativity with customers.

If you go into a supermarket and compare the prices of organic and regular produce, the premiums may surprise you. Many organic products cost 25 to 40 percent more, some are up to double the price. Why are such a fast-growing number of people paying so much more for produce that on the shelf seems similar? The answers to this question can teach us a lot about the true meaning of quality. It is found not just in the products but in the way they are produced, in their certification, and in the supplier–customer relationship. Because so many organic producers cultivate direct contact with their customers, organic consumers have some sense of the people and processes involved in producing the food they are buying, and this personal link is part of the quality in their purchase.

The best test of real quality is the satisfaction of all parties involved in a transaction. It's a feeling as much as a fact. To explore this, look at yourself as a product. Who are your customers? How do your transactions create value for them and for you? Often the emotional value of the exchange counts as much as the tangible benefits.

Pimhill Farm Shop

This is a venture that shows how organic farmers achieve real quality in the complete transaction with their customers, and how organic marketing produces some astute innovations. Pimhill is a 760-acre farm set in the rolling hills of Shropshire, near the English–Welsh border. Owned by the Mayall family since the 1920s, Pimhill was one of the first British farms to go organic, converting in 1949. In those days, the term organic was hardly used and its produce was marketed as compost grown. The Mayalls opened a simple retail outlet on their farm in 1988. By 1997, sales were declining. Ginny Mayall, the third generation of the family to farm at Pimhill, took on responsibility for the shop. She says, "It was clear that we either had to get a lot better or give up. I decided to see how we could make it really outstanding."

One of Ginny's crucial moves was to involve Nick Billet, a Frenchman with a record of successful innovation in several

English hotels and restaurants. Ginny explains, "Nick and I visited the best farm shops we could find, mostly conventional not organic. It was absolutely invaluable having his different expertise alongside mine. Seeing all these places together sparked off a lot of ideas."

What emerged from their weeks of brainstorming is the most attractive and distinctive farm shop I have seen. Everything about the new Pimhill farm shop—the signage, the approach, the building, the internal layout—creates the sense of an enjoyable place for an outing, not just a farm food counter. As Ginny puts it, "We knew we had to make Pimhill worth the trip. Creating a café as part of the farm shop is one of our main ways to do this. Another is to offer a really wide and innovative range of products, including many that you literally can't get anywhere else."

She also notes, "Some of the lines that sell well have been complete surprises to us, and vice versa. We keep experimenting: one of our aims is to offer things other people can't match. We don't conduct formal market research, but everything we do comes from being asked." Among the unique lines and surprise successes are the vegetarian ready meals, which are produced in the Pimhill kitchen when it is not servicing the café.

The sign on the main road outside Pimhill makes no reference to organics. Ginny explains, "I thought mentioning organics would actually put some visitors off. There are still people who think organic food is too specialist or too expensive. Our approach is to draw in as many people as we can. Then we tell them the organic story, let them taste the produce, and realize for themselves that our prices are competitive."

The new Pimhill farm shop and café is a mixture of new and converted buildings, designed by Ginny's architect husband. The total floor area is 12,000 square feet: it clearly represents a major capital investment. The number of customers far exceeds those for the old shop and it is running ahead of budget. Intriguingly, this has been achieved without any advertising. "My previous experience is that it's just not worth it," Ginny says. "Instead we have a form by the checkout and we invite customers to join our free mailing list. This has given us a sizable base of contacts whom we mail regularly about new products and special events like guided farm walks. We also ask customers how they heard of us. Nick and I always reckoned we'd be succeeding if the biggest reason was word of mouth. And it is."

Ginny's approach of responsive experimentation has produced several other marketing initiatives. These include a farm trail, which adds to the "day out" appeal of Pimhill. She has recruited an education officer, who leads guided farm walks for groups of primary school children, geared to themes in the UK's National Curriculum. Charged at £2 per head, these walks cover direct costs and generate sales for the shop and café, plus follow-up visits from families.

The success of the shop and café is now feeding back into the growth of other farm enterprises. To meet the increased demand for vegetables, Pimhill has started a 20-acre market garden, selling to its own shop and delivering to other local outlets. I was impressed by how clearly Ginny and Nick see the need to keep innovating. They know that supermarkets and other competitors will pick up on their ideas, but they have enough creative energy and market awareness to stay ahead of the game.

Real Quality at Work

Imagine it's your birthday and you're going out for a meal with a friend. How would you choose where to go? Would you pay more for this meal than for an average night out? If so, what exactly are you paying the premium for? In our personal lives, we easily recognize and value real quality. We don't pay a premium to get more quantity of food in a fancy restaurant; quite the reverse. The value could be called semi-tangible: the taste of the food, the service, the ambience, the sense of occasion.

Product quality

Numerous consumer studies have been conducted on the motives for buying organic food. Nutrition/health benefits and better taste are generally the main motivations. Product research shows that crops grown organically contain more protein, vitamin C, and valuable trace nutrients. They are typically slower growing and more mature when harvested. The faster-grown, less mature, intensively farmed produce is more watery. There is also a different in durability: organic produce has been shown to stay fresher longer.

With all these advantages, it may seem surprising that organic products have difficulty meeting supermarkets' quality standards. The reason is that the supermarkets focus more on superficial or nominal standards. They believe their sales depend on consistency of shape, size, and freedom from surface blemishes, all of which are easier to achieve with the chemical inputs and suppressants of intensive farming. However, the growth in sales of organic produce shows that more consumers now understand the difference between real quality—taste, nutrition, and satisfaction—and nominal quality.

All the features of real quality on the farm apply in the workplace. In both cases, true quality includes the how and the what of production, the tangibles and intangibles, the emotional and rational benefits. And quality is enhanced by a sense of dialogue and rapport between producer and customer.

Process quality

It is clear that many people now consider the ethics and sustainability of the production process in their purchase decisions. Take as an example the growth in demand for Café Direct coffee and other fair-trade products. Wholesome production is becoming part of the wholesome product, often governed by a certification scheme that ensures credibility.

Another example is the rapid takeup of the Forestry Stewardship Certification scheme by both customers and timber producers. FSC is an independently verified, international assurance scheme for environmentally sustainable timber production. It has been pioneered by the leading British chain of do-it-yourself stores, B&Q, as well as others.

In organic farming, the certification standards are strict and explicit about the methods of production. They include environmental sustainability, animal welfare, wildlife protection, and the health and wellbeing of the people involved. The key organization in British organic farming standards is the Soil Association (SA). This is an extraordinary body, and many industries would benefit from something like it. It fulfills several functions of a producer and a consumer organization, and sustains the trust of both. The SA is a registered charity with around 15,000 members: organic farmers, horticulturalists, and consumers who support organic principles. It speaks for the organic movement as a whole, although its leadership is dominated by active organic farmers. One of its key activities is its certification scheme, which covers over 70 percent of organic production in the UK and checks the standards of overseas suppliers.

The Soil Association has earned its credibility through years of sticking to its principles, even when these reduce the profits of organic producers. This enables it to speak with authority to consumers at large, to journalists, government, supermarkets, and others. With demand for organics growing explosively, juicy price premiums, and conventional farming in desperate straits, the potential for scams, abuse, and mock organic standards is immense. It is largely thanks to the Soil Association that such problems have been rare in the UK.

The production methods in conventional farming can hardly be called high quality in the true sense. Battery chickens are just one example of how many animals are kept in painful, cramped, unnatural conditions. This is not malice: it's what happens when minimum production cost overrides all other considerations.

Conventional farms are pretty unhappy places for people, too. Farmers have one of the highest suicide rates in Britain. The level of occupational health problems and work injuries among farm workers is also high. Imagine working in a highly mechanized dairy parlor, milking 400 cows on your own in two hours. Workers on intensive farms complain of isolation and stress, in much the same language as the workers in a large, automated industrial process.

Although organic farmers and their teams work hard, they mostly seem happy in their work, and their mental and physical health is better than those in conventional farming. Organic methods are more labor intensive, which contributes to job satisfaction and output quality. More of the work is paced by humans, not machines, and more of it involves working with other people. When production processes are naturally aligned and there is real quality of output, you would expect the people involved to feel satisfied and sustainable in their work.

Emotional exchanges

When I introduced the idea of real quality to Salim Hussain at Virosoft, he was both intrigued and perplexed. "My dear chap, you have to remember I'm an engineer," he said wistfully. "For years I've been told: if you can't measure it, it's not real. To me, quality is something you can certify."

I grinned at him mischievously. "OK, but remember our discussion with Aziz? What did he say he most valued about you?"

Salim had his head in his hands, looking even more baffled. "Ahhh... He said he sleeps better at night, he feels reassured by my abilities."

I nodded. "So it's quality assurance, but not as we know it? Think of him as your customer, and you as a supplier. There's a positive emotional exchange between you."

Salim stared at me blankly. "Emotional exchange? What do I get back?"

"Remember we talked about your need for recognition, to have your standing acknowledged?"

"Yes. And sometimes I get that from Aziz."

"Do you ever tell him you want it?"

He looked shocked. "Well, no, I'd be ... embarrassed to say it."

"So how's he supposed to know it's important to you?" Salim was at a loss. I went on, "It's a bit like asking your supplier to guess what your quality spec is."

He looked at me keenly. "Ah, but you said I was the supplier, and he's the customer."

I nodded. "Yes, but real quality is a two-way process. Each party in a sense is both supplier and customer. I mean, Aziz pays you for the services you provide, but I'd say the emotional income you get is more important than the money."

There was a long pause as Salim pondered this. Then he looked up and smiled at me. "Hmm, it's true, the recognition in my work is most valuable to me. And you're right, I'm more likely to get what I want if I specify it. Even if it's qualitative."

"Now what about the people who work for you? Do you tell each other about your quality needs?"

Salim was clearly agitated by this one. He got up, paced around the room, called for a coffee, and at last sat down nervously and looked at me. "This is horrible," he said. "I've been treating them like diodes."

"Diodes? What do you mean?"

"A diode passes current in one direction and not the other. My department is my circuit board. I design the links, I plug the people in, and I just expect them to work. I just couldn't stand to see them as people..."

"Do you know why?" I asked gently.

There was a thoughtful pause. Then he said slowly, "I was afraid if I really listened to their needs, it would overwhelm me. My god, I have people with boyfriends leaving, parents dying. Can I cure these problems?"

"Do they expect you to? Have you asked them?"

He sighed. "No. And maybe recognition is enough."

I went on. "With the people I manage, I keep finding that what I need is the same as what they need. If there's something you want, Salim, ask for it and give it to others, model it."

The concepts of emotional content and exchange gave Salim a kind of engineering framework for human relations in his department. His approach to his people had been much like intensive farming: he applied plentiful inputs of pay, briefs, and deadlines, and expected the output to happen. Now he could see that the personal details his staff had tried to share with him, which he had found irrelevant and uncomfortable, were part of the transaction. As he explained to me, "I used to be afraid that if I met them as people, we'd never get any work done. The whole department would be a chat show and then I'd be jumped on from above. In fact it's the reverse. The productivity has gone up. We're all working better because they can talk to me."

Emotional quality

Whether it's vegetables, cereals, or livestock, most of the produce from a farm has a 70 percent water content. Figuratively, the same could be true for your work outputs: remember that the water element equates to emotional energy. For real quality, the emotional content is essential. In *Blur*, Davis and Meyer are eloquent on this point in the business context:

"Figure out which parts and what proportion of your offer are intangible ... Figure out how to grow the intangibles faster ... When listing your intangibles, include all services ... other forms of information ... and all emotions (which include brand loyalty, customer relationships, employee commitment and the like) ... Remember: every sale is an economic, informational, and emotional exchange ... When you make a sale, be sure you also know what information you want to collect during the exchange and are able to do so. Do the same for emotions. Identify the ones you are selling and the ones you are buying ... Put emotions into every offer and every exchange."

It was from Peter Jansen that I really learned about the emotional aspect of quality and how to cultivate it. Early on at board meetings he chaired, I would sit there perplexed. How did he generate such involvement, such clarity, from everyone? How did he draw out the key issues, and the truth about them, with such ease? The answer had nothing to do with simplistic approaches like "How are we all feeling today?" It had a lot to do with high emotional intelligence, as described by Daniel Goleman in his book *Emotional Intelligence*. This means being articulate and adept in communicating and handling feelings, your own and those of others.

If you apply organic principles, you can develop emotional intelligence and emotional quality. Many of the stories in this book show how openness about feelings develops real quality in working relationships. This links with another lesson from organic farming: the quality of the output grows from the quality of the process. If your ways of working are sustainable, it enriches the end result for you and your customer.

Real Quality in Organizations

If we could monitor the language of companies, the use of the word "quality" would surely have increased a great deal in recent years. Movements like total quality management have increased employees' involvement in the production process and have led to some impressive advances. While they have improved some aspects of real quality, such as product reliability and delivery, they have overlooked others. Organizations are only slowly realizing that the intangibles of real quality can be measured and managed.

The Royal Automobile Club (RAC)

Recently I locked myself out of my car. It was a Saturday lunchtime, I was on my own, and I fortunately had no commitments for the next couple of hours. I was at a large Tesco edge-of-town supermarket. Feeling foolish and upset, I asked at the customer services counter if they had anyone who could help me. Tesco's response was very reassuring. They had an arrangement with the RAC, who would come out and fix the problem for free. They even gave me a voucher for a cup of tea while I waited.

The RAC van arrived within the time promised, 40 minutes. The patrolman was friendly and respectful, competent and resilient. It turned out that my small, basic Vauxhall had been successfully designed to be almost unstealable. The last time I had locked myself out of a car was several years before, at a beach in California. When the breakdown truck arrived, it took literally one minute to get the car open. This time, even with a range of gadgets, it took nearly an hour. I was amazed at the patrolman's composure. I would have been upset by my continuing failure to crack the problem while under the eyes of an agitated customer.

I was equally impressed by the customer satisfaction card he gave me when he finished. The questions on the card showed me that the RAC is an organization that does understand real quality and measures it continually. For example, it asks customers to rate the patrolman for friendliness, calmness, clear explanations, and taking control of the situation. The RAC handles around two million breakdown calls per year. All of these people are given a customer satisfaction card, and 400,000 return them. In 1998, 84.7 percent of these regarded the service as outstanding or better than expected. The RAC clearly recognizes that when your car breaks down, it's not just a mechanical problem, it's an emotionally stressful situation.

Andrew Scotford, the RAC's training manager, comments, "In our recruitment and training, we actually put interpersonal skills and handling the customer's emotional need first. If someone's car breaks down and they have to collect their kids from school, we know the kids are the priority. If our patrol couldn't get the car going immediately, we'd expect them to use the patrol van to help the customer collect the kids. We spend a lot of time teaching our patrols what you could call emotional skills: how to listen, how to reassure, how to resolve conflicting priorities. And we continually monitor our success in meeting these emotional needs through the customer satisfaction card."

Cultivating the opportunity

The ingredients for a shift to real quality standards are present in many organizations. These include quality measurement and feedback systems, the concept of internal customers, and large-scale communications and data-processing technology. All that's missing is a radical change in attitude. The pressure on most organizations for quantified results is acute, so it takes courage to give attention to the intangibles. Yet the business case from organic farming is clear: over time you can build sustained price premiums by delivering real quality benefits such as taste, trust, and rapport.

Many organizations, and the people in them, will need to operate a dual voltage system for quite some time. Especially where supply chains demand tight nominal quality standards, these have to be met alongside intangible values. A mistake some companies make is to create quality for customers without creating it for their own people and processes. As this book explains, real quality arises from ground condition and from the methods of production: it has to apply *within* the organization as well as to customers.

Another lesson from organic farming's success is the need for trustworthy production standards: independently verified, and balancing the needs of the producers, the consumers, and the environment. Creating this will take medium-term vision and unselfishness from the big businesses that shape most production standards. We still lack intermediary bodies that can provide independence in quality standards: organizations with wide consumer membership, willing to engage with producers in developing realistic and trusted quality standards.

Organic Marketing

Organic farmers have evolved a range of distribution methods that are impressive in their quality and ingenuity; all the more so because this is home-grown marketing, it hasn't come from MBAs or management consultants. In marketing as in other areas of organics, the key seems to be the combination of organic principles with a co-creativity that evolves naturally on the job. Although the forms of distribution described here are tailored to foodstuffs, the implications have much wider relevance.

One of the basic principles in organic marketing is to grow value per unit of output, rather than quantity of output.

Farmers achieve this in a number of ways:

❖ Progressively moving into higher-value crops.
❖ Adding value, e.g. salad packs, ready meals, bread, not just ingredients.
❖ Creating distribution methods that increase the producer's share of total transaction value.
❖ Building trust, dialogue, and other intangibles as part of the product value.
❖ Obtaining value from the whole output, so there is no waste.

Another fundamental element of organic marketing is "dialogue distribution," creating channels that enable close, two-way communication between producer and consumer. This dialogue creates resilience, loyalty, and value. A supermarket customer, faced with a product they want being out of stock, may feel angry and go elsewhere. If an organic farm's production is disrupted, dialogue channels enable the farmer to explain the problem and devise a stopgap solution with customers. The dialogue is often an exchange of action as well as words. Farm visits are common, which might include a progress review and discussion of production plans, live education about lambing, helping to pack vegetables, or celebration with a harvest supper.

I see four other principles in organic marketing:

❖ *Locality*: or what organic farmers call local food links. It makes both marketing and environmental sense to trade with the consumers nearest to the source of production. The idea of food miles is steadily gaining consumer awareness: the extraordinary distances a typical piece of food travels between producer, processor, distribution warehouse, supermarket, and consumer. The US average is 1,300 miles.

❖ *Economy*: most organic farmers are undercapitalized, and the blessing in the problem is that they have to develop low-cost approaches.

❖ *Partnership*: both with other producers and with consumers.

❖ *Humanization*: organic marketing actually prefers to add labor content, increase personal contact, and integrate the business and personal aspects of life.

Some examples of these principles in action are outlined below.

Community-supported agriculture (CSA)

This is a major form of organic distribution in the USA, with over 600 active schemes. The approach is also well established in Japan, where it originated. CSA is in effect a joint venture between the producer and the consumer. A group of customers agrees a production plan with an organic grower and contracts to purchase this produce. The customers pay in advance, thus financing the operation, and they share in its risks and rewards. If the harvest is below expectations they receive less food, but they will know why. If the crop is abundant, they share the benefit: more produce, or a share of the income from external sales. CSA schemes stimulate interaction between a farm and its customers. It is common for CSA consumers to provide labor for the operation: some will deal with packing and distributing produce in return for lower prices, some will come as volunteers at busy times just for the fun of it.

Cooperatives

Producer cooperatives have enabled many organic farmers to find the economies of scale for larger marketing or processing initiatives. One of the pioneering British examples is Organic Farm Foods (OFF). This was formed by a group of vegetable producers in a thinly populated area of mid-Wales, who recognized that their local markets were not big enough to support them. They decided to meet the challenge of supplying the supermarkets and created a dedicated packing and distribution operation.

One of the main problems OFF had to overcome was outgrades: usable produce that supermarkets would not accept because of their tight nominal quality demands. OFF processed the outgrades into ready-made salad packs, turning a potentially waste product into an added-value one that helped develop local sales. OFF also found ways to harness the diversity of its members. By tightly coordinating production schedules between them, they were able to provide better continuity of supply for the supermarkets.

Farmers' markets

These have been well established for some time in the USA and are now spreading rapidly in Britain. Like many good innovations, in hindsight the idea seems obvious. Local farmers and growers bring their produce regularly to a downtown venue where consumers can meet them and buy direct. It is a great example of shopping as entertainment and of dialogue distribution. Producers can try out new products and get first-hand feedback on customer needs.

Branded products

A number of kitchen-table attempts to create added-value organic products have grown over the years to successful brands with national distribution. Probably the biggest and best-known of these in the UK is Rachel's Dairy. The appeal of the product is rooted in the superb quality of the milk from Gareth and Rachel Rowlands' herd of Guernsey cows near the Welsh coast. From small beginnings, the product has moved to increasing levels of professionalism in production, packaging, and marketing. At first, sales were purely local, including the Rowlands' farm shop. The brand is now found in many supermarkets nationally, and Rachel's Dairy was acquired in 1998 by a major American producer of organic foods, which intends to expand the output still further.

Customer ownership schemes

This is a term I have coined to describe various arrangements in which the customer is the owner and equity investor in a farming enterprise. Such schemes may involve trade buyers or consumers. In Britain, customer ownership is one of the ways that wholesalers have tackled supply shortages for organic products, especially meat. It is quite common for the wholesaler to supply the livestock for rearing, with the organic farmer receiving a fee and having no financial risk.

There are also some creative examples of consumer ownership schemes. For example, Richard Smith, a farmer near Totnes, wanted to meet the local demand for organic beef, but did not have the funds to start a herd. So he invited the potential consumers to "buy a calf," purchasing the stock that he then reared.

Organic Marketing at Work

How do the innovative marketing and distribution methods of organic farming apply to your work? There are three main principles in these approaches: personal links with customers, dialogue, and cooperation.

The creation of local links and dialogue with customers may seem impractical for large organizations seeking economies of scale. In practice, a great deal can be achieved by combining a genuine service orientation with technology. For example, British Telecom achieves this through customized discount offers on numbers called frequently, as well as personalized account contact by phone.

Information technology enables businesses to accumulate and apply information on the detailed preferences of every customer. Recent innovations in production technology, in a whole range of sectors, make multiple product variations and customization for individuals readily achievable. New approaches to dialogue distribution can harness this scope for customization, ensuring that the producer learns from the customer and that they adapt to changes together.

We can see in organic farming a striking range of joint ventures, some among producers, some between producer and consumer. The message is to move beyond the cult of the competitive, heroic individual. In recent years, even the largest and proudest multinationals have formed webs of cooperative ventures to achieve such benefits as resilience, synergy, and creativity. Each of us can achieve these benefits by increasing collaboration with colleagues and customers.

Real Quality in Daily Practice

Whether you are employed or independent, it helps to see yourself as a product. You need to know who your customers are, how you add value, and how to market yourself. The concepts of real quality and organic marketing can help you achieve this. Imagine yourself as a farm, cultivating a diversity of enterprises, interlinked and mutually supportive.

Cultivate dialogue with your customers and suppliers. Know what real quality means for them. As far as possible, be explicit with them about what you offer and what you need. The more your customers know about how your production processes work, the more loyalty and resilience grows in the relationship. If you work best by going swimming in the afternoons and staying up late, tell them. If you'd like more appreciation to energize you, say so.

Applying this principle begins simply. All you need to do is review the nature of your transactions with your customers and suppliers. Are they fully satisfactory for all of you? Do they contain emotional value? Do you have dialogue and rapport with your supply chain, so that you handle change co-creatively?

The answers to such questions may be less simple. They may deeply challenge your current way of working. This was one reason for the advice in Chapter 1, to read all seven principles before starting a change process. Use the real quality checklist below to develop your vision of the outcome you want. If your way of working is to be truly sustainable, it must deliver real quality: not only for you, but for those with whom you inter-act. Develop your sense of the qualities you want in your work, without trying to define what form or style of work will deliver them. Then use this overall vision to guide your application of all seven principles, starting from ground condition upwards.

Real quality checklist

1 Do you know who your clients are and do you have a direct relationship with them?
(Apply this question to several of your work roles/activities and take time to explore who your key clients/customers are. For example, if you work in a tele-phone call center, your key clients may be your supervisor, his or her boss, and the training and quality managers.)

2 Do you know what real quality means for your key clients? What gives them satisfaction, nutrition, from your work? What emotional value do you deliver in your output?

3 Do your key clients know what real quality means for you? Have you told them what gives you satisfaction and emotional value in your transactions with them?

4 Do the processes by which you personally produce your output embody real quality? In other words, are your ways of working, as well as your outputs, satisfying and wholesome?

5 Do you have a "dialogue relationship" with your clients: a dynamic, two-way relationship that enables both of you to adjust to changes in either party's needs or circumstances?

6 If your answers to questions 1–5 highlight a case for change, list below three steps you can take to begin this.

a

b

c

10
Going
Organic

Conversion is the term used to describe the shift from conventional to organic farming methods. It takes several years of natural cycles and organic cultivation before the ground condition fully recovers its fertility and resilience, and the first two or three years of the conversion period are typically a tough transition. Crop yields, which have depended on artificial fertilizer inputs, usually drop. Because natural predators and the soil's resilience to problems have been suppressed, weeds and pests often get worse before they get better. The main issues in a farm's conversion all have parallels in a human shift to sustainability at work.

This chapter's focus is the practicalities of moving toward sustainability. It offers guidelines condensed from my personal experience, from Magdalen Farm, and from clients with whom I have worked.

Alison Martin, the middle manager in the NHS whose story was described earlier in the book, has been persistent in bringing sustainable principles to her work, and her experience is illuminating (some of the tools she mentions are included in Chapter 11):

"It must be over two years now since I went on the first workshop about The Natural Advantage. I was in a pretty bad way then: successful at work, but terribly wound up about it, and it was knocking hell out of my health and my personal life. I didn't know much about sustainability then, but I had some sense that it was relevant to my problems.

"As soon as I did the personal energy audit, the whole thing was obvious. I could see that my way of working was depleting me and I was getting by with a load of quick-fixes that only made it worse. That conversation with Peter Norman about sending in the pigs was such an eye-opener. Ever since, one of the ways I've made this approach work for me is to keep using the image of myself as a farm, a piece of earth, as a way of seeing what I need.

"I came away from that workshop at Magdalen determined to change things, but I plunged in too quickly, which is what I usually do. I remember Alan talking about planning the conversion phase, but I didn't. I was in a bit of a panic about my health, to be honest.

"I knew that in the conversion stage things would probably have to get messier before they straightened out, and that was true in my case. When I started facing the feelings I'd been stuffing down, I was in turmoil for several months. I had weekly counseling sessions through all that time, and they were invaluable. The connected breathing and composting were really useful when I got swamped with feelings at work, and in the first few weeks that happened almost every day. Usually I'd just excuse myself and go for a 10-minute walk around the block and that was enough time to clear it.

"I did talk a bit about this to my boss and she was pretty

understanding. I didn't go into details, but I told her I needed to change my working style and personal habits because my health was suffering. What we set up for the first couple of months, which helped me a lot, was a short weekly review. She'd tell me her immediate priorities and I'd warn her if I was having a really bumpy week.

"One of the things that helped me a lot with the conversion phase was the idea of real quality. I liked the way that organic farmers have more of a personal relationship with their customers, so there's a kind of mutual adjustment to change. A lot of my work was easy to do impersonally and that's how I'd preferred it. I was bloody efficient, but you wouldn't have wanted to know me. I was burning myself out in the effort to avoid any risk of criticism. After the Magdalen session, I let myself develop a bit of a personal relationship with my main work contacts. If I was feeling exhausted, I'd actually tell them so and negotiate deadlines instead of saying yes to everything.

"I guess seeing Peter Norman's way of working at Magdalen Farm helped me, as did this idea of co-creativity. It's not so orderly, more a sort of productive flux, but it's more human and a lot more adaptable. I started to get quite a lot of appreciation from my work colleagues about the way I'd changed. Even if I was a moody so-and-so, we learned how to handle it. I'd say the basic conversion period for me was about six months. After that, things were on a fairly even keel at work and my personal life felt sustainable too.

"A few months after that, I had a very good annual appraisal from my boss—and then I was made redundant a couple of months later. So it came as a hell of a shock, it felt like a real kick in the teeth when I felt I'd just learned how to do the job well without exhausting myself. It showed me I still had a lot more to learn. Not just about diversity, but also about adapting to far more change and less security. I must admit, even with what I'd learned from The Natural Advantage, I was quite depressed and angry for a few months after the redundancy. Then I went back to basics and worked on my ground condition.

"This time, I did plan things better. I used the Diamond Process to figure out the work I wanted, what kind of farm I'd like to be. For a start, I could see that I need both security and variety, so I had to find the synergy between them.

"My main work now is managing the membership department of a large mail-order business. It uses my previous experience, and the great thing is I'm doing it three days a week. It's a very commercial business, much more fast moving than the National Health Service, but I can manage it fine on this part-time basis. One thing I realized I've always missed in my work is physical activity and contact with nature. These days, I do voluntary work one day a week with a non-profit group called Therapeutic Gardens. We create and maintain gardens for people who are partially sighted or mentally handicapped. It's about the best renewal crop I could imagine for myself."

Conversion on the Farm

As Francis Blake comments in his book *Organic Farming and Growing*. "The first step in the conversion of a farm is the conversion of the farmer. There are two requisites. The first is a change in your attitude and your thinking ... You will need to get away from the conventional approach to any problem ... that of seeking to dominate it by using outside inputs—and instead cultivate the ability to look at it in the context of the rest of the farm, to see behind the problem to what is causing its undue development ... Look at the farm as a whole, for each part has an influence on everything else.

"The second requisite is a belief in your own mind that the organic approach is the right one. In order to feel confident and positive about this new direction, so that you can carry it through even in the difficult times and against the barracking of your neighbours, then you have to put your faith in it ... Without that whole-hearted belief, there is no room for the development of either the pioneering spirit or the understanding that organic farming requires for its successful operation."

Every word of this applies as much to the workplace as the farm.

Generally, it is easier to convert a farm if you have operated it conventionally for a year or more before moving to organic methods. That way, you already know the farm's characteristics: the typical weed and pest threats, what crops grow best, how it reacts to different weather conditions. In contrast, we started conversion as soon as we bought Magdalen farm: the result was two years of continual surprises. The analogy for your work is to know yourself well before you embark on a change of this scale. In the same way, in my consultancy with Alibi Publishing and Virosoft, I sought to build trust and understanding in the team before we considered sustainability.

When conversion gets underway, restoring ground condition and raising fertility are the fundamental issues. You have to create the conditions for growth. Most farms start the conversion phase from a state of depletion. In the first year or two, the emphasis goes to less demanding, less valuable, renewing crops such as grass or clover pasture. It is also common to import some extra fertility to restimulate the soil and speed up the process of renewal. Under organic standards, some manure, seaweed, and other natural minerals can be brought in when necessary.

In the first year of organic production, output volumes are likely to be below previous levels. After years of neglect, it takes time for the soil to come back to life as an organism and produce its own fertility. Weed problems also tend to be bad at the start, before the natural system's checks and balances come into play. These early weeds are like the turbulence we find in many transitions: along with our desire to change, there may be some fear and resistance within us and from those around us.

Although the volume of production may drop, the value per unit should rise. It usually takes two years of conversion before a farm and its produce qualify as organic, but during this period, they qualify for "in conversion" status. The high demand for organic produce means that even the conversion-grade produce earns a premium over conventional farm goods. So don't panic if the volume of your output drops during the transition: value the quality, and seek customers who will do likewise.

Easing the stress

An organic farmer knows that the conversion period is likely to be stressful. Production outputs and money income are at risk. There is a huge amount to learn and many of the issues can't be anticipated: they will be met in the moment. Every farm is unique to some degree and at best you can embark on this voyage with a rather generalized map.

There are many ways to mitigate this stress in your own conversion process. One is simple awareness: make sure that you, your colleagues, customers, family, and friends know the scale of the change and are ready to support it. Another is to set up some sort of financial cushion, so you can take off the pressure to maintain your output.

A further way to reduce the stress of conversion is by planning. The pioneers of organic farming had to proceed by trial and error; nowadays, the conversion process is well researched and there are specialist consultants who can help you to apply this experience to your situation. Of course, conversion cannot be fully planned: some issues can be forecast and quantified, but many can't. Producing a conversion plan is certainly helpful, but it needs to be reviewed frequently and there has to be willingness to change it substantially as the process unfolds. The same is true of the transition to human sustainability, whether it is on the personal, team, or organizational level.

Lessons from Magdalen

What have I learned about sustainability from nine years' involvement with Magdalen Farm? The grand answer is that sustainability is more a journey than a destination. The humble answer is that we're not there yet! Magdalen completed its initial conversion to organic methods in 1992 and the farm has met organic production standards since then. However, the farm has faced several changes that have led to some of the conversion challenges coming round again, much like repetitions of the competence cycle described in Chapter 7.

When I look back at the original conversion that Dirk Hoostra and I managed, I feel we did pretty well. It was often tough and surprising, but we had a good framework. The professional support from Mark Measures, our organic farming adviser, was excellent: the conversion plan he produced with us provided a sound overall action plan and budget. Having Norman Hale as a local friend, and his well-established organic farm as a role model, was also invaluable. The toughest part of the whole process was to get two hard-driving bulls, Dirk and myself, to learn co-creativity. We both wasted a lot of time and emotion before we learned to work with the problems instead of trying to wrestle them to the floor.

When Dirk and Marika returned to the Netherlands in 1994, bringing in new farmers was a bit like starting over. The same was true when John and Anna Woodward moved on and Peter Norman joined us, three years later. Peter was our first fully qualified and experienced farm manager and he showed us that significant changes were required to make Magdalen sustainable in the full sense.

Market conditions had altered greatly since we started and our 20-cow dairy herd was no longer economic. We also knew that the size of the farm, 130 acres, was small for a commercially viable enterprise. We set up a joint venture agreement with Peter that enabled him to invest some personal capital to start new enterprises and expand the farm by renting 50 acres of organic land nearby. As a result, Magdalen now has a bigger number of enterprises and ones where our scale of production should be competitive. Peter and his partner Christina have also addressed a major deficiency by bringing in organic marketing methods. We now have a good local customer base, with dialogue and diversity. Previously, most of the produce had been sold to one or two large national customers and no personal relationship had existed.

I recently asked Peter if he regarded Magdalen Farm as sustainable yet. He replied, "It's pretty good and improving, but there's a way to go in several areas. The environmental sustainability is fair, but we're not yet humanly sustainable. The farm team is working longer hours and feels more stretched than I'd like. But we're only in the second year with a lot of the new enterprises, and each annual cycle should get a lot easier. We're not financially sustainable yet, either. We're still in the start-up phase: we expected losses last year and we lost more than I thought we would. Some of the learning was quite expensive. This year's a lot better: I should be able to pay myself this year and next year should show a decent profit."

I hope that this account of the Magdalen experience underlines the point that sustainability is not some nirvana of stability, a never-never land where nothing needs to change any more. In fact, it's more like the concept of bounded uncertainty from chaos theory: turbulent, but in a constructive way. What I can also see by reviewing nine years of organic growth at Magdalen is how applying sustainable principles increases resilience and the capacity for change. As Peter says, "The two farmers before me helped to renew ground condition and establish an organic foundation I could build on. Starting three major enterprises in the same year was seriously ambitious, and I've depended on the resources in the land to support me."

Conversion at Work

If you are ready to convert to sustainable principles in your work, should you expect two years of turmoil? Probably not: human beings are capable of much greater and quicker adaptation than a farm. Your productive output may not drop at all, but it is wise to be prepared for it to do so. Accept that going organic is not a plug-and-play move, it is a cyclical process. You will learn and embody the principles of sustainability by using them repeatedly. As you manage your energy and your work in cycles, you move through the conversion process to the stage where applying organic principles becomes habitual and intuitive, and renewal is a natural process.

So how do you make the switch? This section offers you two kinds of answer. The first is 16 pointers for your transition phase, drawn from my own experience and others with whom I have worked. The second is specific suggestions on how to develop a conversion plan, drawing on the analogy with organic farming.

Making your transition

1 You don't have to wait. You don't need the world or your employer to reach a crisis on this issue before you make your move. Even if you work in a culture that tends to deplete people, you can operate on dual voltage and do a great deal to sustain yourself.

2 You don't have to do it alone. Remember how collaborative organic farmers are. There are organizations and individuals who can support you with this change and from whose experience you can learn.

3 It is better to act on feeling than on fact. By the time the problem is categorically proven, it may be too late to resolve it. If you sense that your work is depleting you, even if you don't know it for sure, act on the feeling.

4 If in doubt, intensify the problem. Exaggerate your feelings, caricature the situation, use humor to open it up. Apply the composting principle. Go deeper into the creative tension. Keep believing that the gift is in the problem.

5 Work with the profit motive, not against it. You may feel angry that the economic system exploits you, but don't start from there. Finding synergy with the organization's needs will get you further. As an individual, you're not big enough to confront the system, but by aligning your nature with its needs you can reshape it.

6 Start with principles—and stick with them. You're initiating a major change and the form of the outcome is hard to guess. Use the principles from this book or shape your own. Either way, the principles of sustainability are your compass and your fudge detector.

7 You don't have to jump off a cliff. You can't plan every detail of a change like this, but you can plan for it, just as a farm does. Learn from others' experiences before you start. Recognize your needs and risks, emotional and practical. Line up the resources and support you may need. And keep your plan co-creative: review and replan as you progress.

8 Anchor the ends of the cycle and the middle will follow. Focus your attention on your ground condition and on the full, real quality of your outputs, for yourself and your cus-

tomers. Getting these right should naturally move you into the whole cycle of sustainability.

9 Find allies. Look out for the individuals and groups, within your work and outside it, who can develop sustainability with you. If you can avoid getting evangelical, you may find your colleagues surprisingly receptive. Often when I have helped a team to explore this issue, the comment afterwards has been: "I never knew so many of us shared these values."

10 Be a trailblazer. A change like this has to involve risk. You can reduce it and cushion it, but you can't eliminate it. The whole area of human sustainability at work is a pioneering one: by exploring it, you serve not only yourself but others who can learn from you.

11 Create standards. The conversion period is usually messy. The pressure and clarity of immediate profit and performance goals can feel hard to counterbalance. Develop a standard, a way to measure your progress or otherwise, for each of your sustainable principles. Don't worry if your standards are home grown. And if they're qualitative, so much the better!

12 Pack lunch. Gather your resources before you start the journey. Give time to cultivating your ground condition, building up your resources and resilience, before you start the conversion process.

13 Transform your energy productivity. The catchphrase "work smarter, not harder" has been around for years. Organic principles offer the way to do this substantially and sustainably. As you combine your brainpower with natural cycles, and as you consciously manage your energy levels, you create the potential for dramatic rises in the value created per unit of your energy. Carry a vision of doing more with less and look for the synergies to achieve it.

14 Find your market. Believe that there are customers who will value real quality as you develop it, and persist until you find them. They may even be your current clientele.

15 Celebrate. When most people lived and worked on the land, celebrating the seasons and cycles was widespread. Marking and enjoying your progress through your cycles will help to sustain you. It's probably the seasons you find hardest that you most need to celebrate!

16 Remember to renew. Both the mechanistic mindset and the culture of the hero-achiever may make you think that the only way to get progress is to push. In fact most heroes, from Odysseus to Batman, are highly co-creative: they know when to push, but also when to retreat, rest, review, receive. You will need persistence to make this change, but that means knowing when to stop as well as when to keep going. And if you become depleted or frustrated, don't be tough on yourself: go back to principles and see how to renew your resources.

Making a Conversion Plan

If you want to work sustainably, planning the transition phase is worth the effort. It's a good way to consolidate and apply your understanding of all seven principles as a whole. The idea of a plan may sound rather fixed and formal: treat it as a framework for co-creativity, a way of clarifying your intent before you plunge into the flow of events. The Diamond Process described in Chapter 6 is a good way to develop your plan, so that your intuition and analytical talents are both involved. Treat the topics and questions below as suggestions for possible inclusion in your plan. Tailor your own format and contents to your taste and your circumstances.

Ground condition survey

What is the state of your underlying resources? How fertile or depleted are you currently? Are your four energy elements each at a good level and in balance as a whole? If your ground condition is poor, explore how to renew it systematically: in other words, address the root causes. Rebuild structure and fertility in a way that moves you toward a sustainable balance of energy inputs and outputs.

Energy sources

Use the Personal Energy Audit to identify current and potential energy inputs to your work. Consider sources within you and around you. Notice any imbalances and deficiencies and plan how you can address them. The level of energy inputs you can access will directly influence your level of productive potential. If you are physically fit, bathed in support from colleagues, mentally alert, and inspired by the corporate vision, it will make a difference! Remember that waste is a potential major energy source.

Soil type and potential

Look back at the section on soil types in Chapter 2, and if possible identify your type: for example sand, clay, or loam. By considering this alongside your data on ground condition and energy sources, you can explore your productive potential. What kind of crops will suit you best? What mix of enterprises will be renewing and resilient for you?

For example, if you are a chalky soil type, with low reserves and limited energy sources, you need to consider relatively simple, undemanding crops, or you will deplete yourself. On the other hand, if you are a loam type, with good energy sources (including waste), you can aim for higher-value, more demanding crops, but you should still alternate these with renewal crops and ensure that energy flows are balanced.

Market review

Having considered the production side of the equation, it's now time to look at sales. By now you may know what you can produce—but what can you sell, and what do you *want* to sell? Apply the principles of Chapter 9. Consider both current and potential products, and present and potential customers. Where is the best prospect of achieving real quality and an on-going relationship, both for you and your customers?

At this stage, it may be useful to explore different options and create some scenarios. For example, one could be a low-output plan: if your sustainable production level seems low, can you adjust to lower financial income but earn it through crops that are satisfying in other ways? Alternatively, if you want to continue in a high-output, demanding occupation, can you invest some of your earnings to increase your energy inputs and support to sustainable levels?

Work–life balance

Tradeoffs between the areas of work and life are worth considering explicitly. For example, you may choose to stay in a depleting job and meet the deficit by drawing support from your family. You may opt for this because it provides enough income to support your family in the lifestyle you all want. Often we make such decisions alone, heroically. The most resilient way to make such a choice is through open discussion with those involved, so they can agree and support the work–life balance you decide on. Here too, it may be worth considering different scenarios.

Vision

This should be a good stage to turn to intuition and inspiration to show you the best choice among various priorities and options. If some of your goals seem incompatible with each other, remember to use this creative tension, to look for the synergy between them. Creating Your Farm, the exercise at the end of this section, offers you one method to explore this further.

Evaluation/action plan

When you have a vision that feels right, you can evaluate it against the practical issues you have already identified. Can you produce this vision sustainably? Will it bring in the money and satisfaction you want from your work? Is it resilient to change? Does it balance your work and personal life? If your overview is positive, you can check it out in detail by preparing an action plan, including the points below.

Energy budget

An organic farm will budget the flows of a key nutrient like nitrogen to ensure that fertility is not depleted. Although the key human energy flows are intangible, you can guesstimate inflows and outflows using a format like the Personal Energy Audit. This is a good sanity check on your vision, to assess if your available energy inputs will meet the demands renewably.

Maintenance

Compare a Grand Prix car with a family saloon. The racing car delivers extraordinary performance, but must have large, frequent inputs of labor and materials to keep it on the road. Err on the side of conservatism in assessing the maintenance and support you need for your work. The risks from overproviding are relatively low. Be clear what you need and negotiate it with those around you. If you need to play snooker with your pals three nights a week to handle a difficult job, ask your partner if he or she is willing to accept the equation. Much of your support may come from yourself, friends, family, and colleagues, but look seriously at the idea of paying for professional support too.

Financial budget

A budget is essential to a farm conversion plan. There will be new items of spending, as well as savings, different income sources, and more uncertainty. One of the reasons for budgeting is to quantify the financial risks in the conversion phase and provide contingency funds to cover them. If you can do the same for your own transition, it can reduce the stress of the change for you and those close to you.

Measurement and review

How will you know if your plan is succeeding: when and how will you review your progress? One of your motives for this change is presumably to improve your wellbeing, so find some benchmarks, however qualitative they are. More tangible measures are also useful, such as hours worked, and regular Personal Energy Audits.

I strongly advise setting up a regular review cycle, perhaps weekly or monthly, as a way of steering and sustaining your change. During the Magdalen Farm conversion, we had quarterly reviews with our professional adviser. A periodic review of your plan with a friend, counselor or mentor can give you an objective view and the benefit of wider experience.

Creating Your Farm

This exercise helps you use the farm analogy to develop the future direction of your work. Choose a quiet, comfortable place to do this, and have some plain paper and colored pens.

Picture you and your work roles as if you were a farm. What kind of farm would you like to become? Imagine that you are a landscape, a range of fields, facilities, enterprises: a network of fruitful flows and cycles, earning the income you need, and enhancing your underlying resources as you do so.

You can use this analogy literally or figuratively. Picture your work as actual farm enterprises: cereals, vegetables, cows, and so on, and then see what they symbolize for you. Or explore how your work roles could evolve so that they are productive, synergistic, diverse, and sustainable like an organic farm.

Either way, remember that the future of a farm is shaped by its past and present. What are your soil type and ground condition? What crops have you grown well, which customers already value you? And what history of weeds and pests do you have to learn from?

Spend some time daydreaming about these questions, feeling receptive to new images. As they arise, start drawing them, creating a picture of the farm you would like to be.

Toward Natworking

With many innovations, widespread uptake is preceded by a wilderness phase when a few people see the need and the solution, but general opinion is still blinkered. This is how many of us experienced organic farming until the mid-1990s. I see the concept of human sustainability as being in the same position now, although I am optimistic that this will change over the next few years. A scenario of how it may change is given in the Epilogue: Three Healing Crises.

I have coined the term "natworking" to describe ways of working that embody natural principles and that are both productive and humanly sustainable. If you choose to develop a natworking approach in your work, you will be helping create the ground condition for this idea to grow into the mainstream. And as these ideas take root with more individuals and organizations, the process of conversion becomes easier.

Conversion in Organizations

How does an organization become humanly sustainable? Frankly, I'm not sure. I can't point to a company that fully embodies all these principles, but I can offer both ideas and the results of some pilot work. Working organically is not an easy proposition for most organizations: although it offers the prospect of higher-value output and improved performance, results will be less controllable. This is a hard risk for any manager to take when the pressure for constant results is so strong.

The way that other innovations start and spread may offer a model for this one: often the early experiments are likely to be in smaller, privately owned companies, and a handful of larger, progressive groups, probably in one of their wild-margin subsidiaries. As a body of experience gathers, conversion processes evolve, the benefits to customers and employees become apparent, and demand grows.

Most of the pointers in this chapter about individual conversion are also relevant to organizations and teams. There is the same risk of trying to do the right thing, but too soon and in the wrong way. The first step is ground condition: roots, not fruits. A group needs to develop its skills and culture, as well as understanding and motivation, before moving into the maximum growth phase. I have described below the experience of one organization I have worked with, which was profiled earlier.

Alibi Publishing

Our work with Alibi proved sustainable and survived the appointment of a new chief executive. I asked Steve Raleigh, Alibi's human resources director, to give his account of the conversion process:

"That first workshop we did with Alan and Barry was quite remarkable. I've been on a lot of workshops and I'm pretty

skeptical, but this one really had a lasting effect. All the principles and skills they presented were related to our needs, both
personal needs and the business situation. The team had bought
into the fact that Phil, our chief executive, would be moving on
so we were really hungry for a solution. What we realized from
that first workshop was that no one could prescribe the answer:
we had to make the solution ourselves, but they gave us the
tools to do it.

"The few weeks after that first workshop were quite strange,
and quite funny really. Mostly we were doing it differently and
seeing that it worked. Every now and then one of us, usually
Phil, would fall back into old habits. He'd start answering the
question as soon as he'd posed it, and the rest of us would just
stare at him. Usually, he stopped in mid-sentence and ground
his teeth while the rest of us got messy and co-creative, and
eventually found an answer. At least he admitted that our
answer was sometimes better than his.

"Having the second workshop without Phil was brilliant.
What still amazes me about that session is the honesty. There
are quite a lot of power struggles within our team and I would
never have imagined we could talk openly about them in the
whole group. But we did. It certainly proved out this composting idea. After that, we realized that being open about our conflicts is tremendously energizing. And we'd learned enough of
the skills to start doing it with our subordinates.

"At that second workshop, we knew that Phil's move was
imminent, and we had a gutsy, straight-out talk about how we
were going to manage the business as a group of peers. We also
wanted to do it without having Working Vision or anyone else
holding our hand all the time. The question of how to do this
sustainably was a good point of reference. Simon, our quality
director, and I are accepted as neutral parties in the power struggles, so we acted as mediators when people couldn't solve their

own disputes. When Phil was moved to Germany, we had several months without a boss and managed remarkably well. His successor, Wolfgang, is an engineer. He spent time understanding why we'd worked so well, and he bought into the approach.

"I know that Alan has developed his ideas further since they worked with us, and I don't think we're applying all of his model here. The stuff about ground condition, composting and co-creativity has helped us a lot. We still have to deal with the output pressure from Germany, but we have enough freedom over here to work out our own ways of doing it.

My advice to a company considering The Natural Advantage model would be this: go for it, but make it your own before you start. Adapt it and tailor it to your situation, your culture. Spend time exploring it and building up ground condition before you really launch it. Otherwise it'll be what we call a Chinese-dinner initiative: the whole bright idea will be through the system and out the other end before you've had time to digest it. The other thing I'd say is that you don't have to go deep into the farming analogy to use this process. We just called it working naturally."

Conversion in Daily Practice

Perhaps the best advice I can offer is to echo the remarks above: explore these ideas, adapt them for yourself, and gradually develop your ground condition before you take it further. The best way to do this is cyclically: reread the book and see how the principles support each other as you consider how to apply them to your situation.

I have found that for myself and many others, the principles of *The Natural Advantage* make intuitive sense, so they take root easily. I have been applying this approach in my work and personal life for the past three years. It has been a time of difficult change as well as high productivity, and I know that my reserves and resilience are much higher now than when I started. I have learned that working sustainably can be turbulent and sometimes chaotic. My habitual need for control is greatly reduced: most of the time I can handle uncertainty and use it productively. I still get tired and stressed in my work quite often, but I move through it fast and usually find the learning in the problem quickly.

If I were to offer three keys to conversion they would be these:

❖ Look after your ground condition.
❖ When it gets sticky, get co-creative.
❖ Keep aiming for real quality: satisfaction for you and your customers.

11
The Organic Growth Toolkit

This chapter offers you some processes to supplement those in the rest of the book. These further tools are especially relevant to cultivating organic synergy, co-creativity, and composting, but since these are central to the whole approach of *The Natural Advantage*, they will help you apply all seven principles.

The principles in *The Natural Advantage* are interdependent. If you have started to nourish your ground condition, harness natural energy, and compost your energy waste, you are already enhancing your co-creative abilities. And as you develop your co-creativity further, this will move you toward embodying all the other principles.

The Witness Triangle

This is a way of exploring two positions or drives that are in tension and moving to a third point. The exercise uses physical movement and visualization to help you stay with tension, and find the synergy in it.

Preparation

Begin by clarifying your intent, the outcome you want from this process. Then review the various issues and factors involved in the situation. Focus on the main tension or uncertainty that is holding you back from making a clear, easy decision. If possible, identify the primary pull, the underlying tension or conflict you need to resolve. Often this is between a "yes" and a "but": desire for action, and resistance to it. The process here is written for this kind of conflict, but can be adapted for others.

One way to use the Witness Triangle is to ask someone to read the following guidelines for you, stopping when you give a signal, to ensure that you go at your own pace. If this is not possible, ask someone to record it on tape for you or do this yourself. Alternatively, read the instructions through several times and take yourself through them from memory.

Process

Sit comfortably, take some long, deep, slow breaths, relaxing into any tension you are feeling. Place your hands in a comfortable position, apart from each other, and with the palms facing upward, fingers relaxed and in an open position.

Now, focus your attention on your right hand, and in relation to the question you are exploring, feel the "yes" side of the equation. Sense the desire, the drive in you toward this outcome. Imagine you have already achieved this outcome: let yourself feel how this is for you. Savor the satisfaction fully.

Sense the energy of all this and let it focus and gather in your right hand.

Now, move your attention to your left hand. As you continue to picture the "yes" side fully, let your awareness of the "but" side emerge. What are your fears, doubts, uncertainties about this move? Let them express themselves fully: give them an attentive hearing. If you feel tension rising as you do this, breathe deeply, keep relaxing into it: believe you will soon find the synergy between these sides of the question. Let yourself feel the force of your resistance and focus this in your left hand. If your attention starts to wander, bring yourself back to the sensations in your hands and the rest of your body.

Now, move your attention to a third point, the witness position. Focus your attention on the "third eye" point in the center of your forehead. From this place, witness the power and the energy in both your right and left hands. Feel the tension vividly, but know that you are bigger than this conflict: you encompass it, you can witness it and find the purpose in it. Start slowly moving your hands together. Keep your breathing deep, embrace this tension as creative and positive. Continue bringing your hands together and breathing into the tension. Stay with this until you get a sense of an answer emerging.

The Aikido Approach

Co-creativity and synergy may seem like abstract concepts. It can be useful to have a visual map, like the Diamond, or a physical embodiment, which is what aikido offers. The word "aikido" literally means "the way of blending energy": it is a Japanese martial art based on the principle of using conflicting forces constructively. I first met aikido through a workshop led by Thomas Crum in 1990, and it was here that I was introduced to the concept of co-creativity. Tom's all-American win-or-die attitude to competitive sport had been demolished when he was floored by an aikido expert far smaller and older than him. He has written a book, *The Magic of Conflict*, on applying aikido principles in life and work.

Imagine someone is attacking you, trying to punch you in the chest. An aikido response would be to turn through 90 degrees and step slightly to the side, so that the attacker's fist is traveling past you, not into your chest, and then to move with the energy and direction of the attack. As you move with it, you can use your energy, strength, and intention to steer the attack away from you and in a different direction: in effect, finding the third way that is crucial in any co-creative process.

It takes training and discipline to respond to conflict in this way. The principles by which aikido engenders this ability are well described in Thomas Crum's book. The main ones are summarized below.

Staying aware

Imagine the attack scene again. To handle it successfully, you need your full powers of attention and observation on what is actually happening: your response must arise from them. If you get into worries, fears, or theories, you'll be on the floor. With practice and as you become more centered, you can discover a remarkable sense of spaciousness, of time slowing down, and the ability to see fully, even in a situation where the other person is moving quickly, with an aggressive emotional charge.

Conflict is not competition

Many people, especially men, are conditioned to see conflict as a win–lose situation—they must either prevail or be humiliated. Phil Morris, profiled in Chapter 3, is an example of this. The more you can see conflict as an interesting, instructive opportunity, and the less you prejudge it on your fears and beliefs, the better.

Stay centered

In aikido, as in tai chi and many eastern disciplines, you need to be centered at all levels: physical, emotional, mental, and spiritual. Physically, this means keeping your awareness focused on the *hara*, your physical center of gravity, in the abdomen below the navel. When I tried this in Tom's workshop, I discovered that this makes it hard for anyone to push you off balance. Another aspect of staying centered is the ability to embody "fluid power": to be strong yet fluid like a fire hose, not tense and brittle like a stick. This is the principle of relaxing into tension while maintaining active awareness.

Flow to outcome

This is what Tom calls the key co-creative stage. In all the conflict resolution training I have led, letting go of attachment to the form of the outcome is a crucial learning point. It is appropriate to have a vision of a desired result but to carry it lightly: envision the qualities and the essence of an outcome, and don't hold on to them. Let go and be fully present in the flow of the process. Doing so creates the scope for the right-brain leap, the synergistic solution.

Connected Breathing

You can do this exercise throughout the day, whenever you feel the need. It helps with general relaxation and alertness, and can also be used in composting.

❖ Take four short breaths.
❖ Then take one long breath.
❖ Pull the breaths in and out through the nose.
❖ Do four sets of five breaths—that is, four sets of four short breaths followed by one long breath without stopping—for a total of 20 breaths.

❖ Merge the inhale with the exhale so the breath is connected without any pauses. All 20 breaths are connected in this manner, so you have one series of 20 connected breaths with no pauses.

❖ On the inhale, consciously draw the breath in with a relaxed manner. Let go completely on the exhale, while continuing to keep the inhale and exhale the same length.

❖ Use short breaths to emphasize the connecting and merging of the inhale and the exhale into unbroken circles.

❖ Use the long breath to fill your lungs as completely as you comfortably can on the inhale and to let go completely on the exhale.

❖ Breathe at a speed that feels natural for you. It is important that the breathing be free and natural and rhythmical, rather than forced or controlled.

Since most of us have developed bad breathing habits you might initially experience some physical sensations, such as light-headedness or tingling sensations in your hands or elsewhere.

Negative Energy Recycling

This exercise is adapted with permission from one developed by the Hoffman Institute.

Identify

Most of us have a lot of negative energy trapped in repeating patterns of feelings, beliefs, and behavior. Begin this process by identifying a pattern you want to transform.

❖ *Example*: After yet another disagreement with my boss, I realize that I have a repeating pattern of responding to conflict by withdrawal. I become cold and aloof: this freezes out any possibility of finding a constructive solution, and leaves me feeling angry and tense inside. I realize that this pattern occurs in many of my relationships.

Relive the pattern

Relive a recent problem situation in which you demonstrated this negative pattern. How are you behaving? Get in touch with what it's doing to you. How do you feel? Where do you feel the pattern in your body? Place your hand there.

Transform

Visualize the negative pattern as having a tangible form and shape. Imagine removing it from your body and holding it in your hands. Start to work with the negative trait as you have visualized it, physically moving your hands as if you were handling a ball of clay. While you do so, picture transforming this negative pattern into pure energy. Sometimes this will happen quickly, sometimes you may have to persist for a while.

Keep your hands apart from each other, visualizing the negative trait between them. Increasing the speed of movement of your hands can help. Now rub your hands together rapidly and visualize this pure energy expanding into a ball of shining light energy. Let your hands move slightly apart, still feeling the power of the energy between them.

Look inside this ball and see a message written just for you. Typically it will be a message about how to redefine and recycle the negative pattern. For example, if I am processing my withdrawal pattern, the message might be "stay present and say how you feel."

Now hold the ball containing your message above your head and let it descend slowly as it enters your body. Allow yourself to feel and experience the sensation being created in you by this energy. Feel this new sensation fill your body.

Experience

With this sensation inside you, go back to the original problem. This time, as you relive the situation get in touch with what you are thinking, how you are feeling and how you are responding. Let this be the feeling that replaces the old one and relates to new, positive types of behavior.

Creative Conflict Resolution

This is a process that I have developed, partly based on Edward de Bono's book *Conflicts*. It is designed so that you can learn and apply it in real time, without having to keep reading the instructions. It's an effective way of bringing mental heat and light to emotional situations, as relevant for conflicts within you as for conflicts with others.

In most cases, conflict is made more bitter by two factors: the emotional content and our beliefs about conflict. Our sense of face, our sense of our own identity and self-worth, often feels as if it is fundamentally challenged by a conflict. This is where the intense emotions of anger, fear, and pain arise, and we can easily see ourselves in a fight for our survival, because the emotional level has taken over. Often the current issue carries old emotions from past issues. It is important to understand repeating patterns: for example, if I was let down when I was younger, I am likely to have repeated experiences of betrayal and letdown throughout my life, and they will bring up feelings of intense anger that are out of proportion to the immediate provocation. At least, they will do so until I recognize the repeating pattern and start to choose to react otherwise.

Until we understand the pattern of carrier emotions, we risk getting sucked into escalating every conflict. We risk believing that all of our emotions are about the immediate issue. We also risk believing that all the emotion expressed by the other party in the conflict is aroused by and directed at us personally, instead of making allowances for their carrier emotions. The other factor hampering us is our beliefs about conflict. We often see it as a fight, a battle to be won or lost. We believe that our personal self-worth is at stake if we "lose."

Creative conflict resolution is a three-step process to defuse a situation, develop understanding, and find constructive solutions. The three stages are: cooling, clarifying, and constructing.

Cooling

There are three needs to be met during this stage.

Accept the emotions involved as valid and let them be expressed

In the early stages of a conflict, when the tension and heat are rising rapidly, each party typically feels that they are not heard by the other. This may be literally true, in that people are denying that there is a conflict and are avoiding facing it; or it may be true in the sense that each party is so preoccupied with their own feelings that they don't truly hear anyone else. Without structure, this heat is often intolerable for one or both parties. Intense emotions are like boiling water or steam: dangerous, powerful, and hard to handle. The heat needs to be managed, to use the tension and bring the temperature in the conflict to a level where progress is possible. Although I have called this stage cooling, it is a composting process and therefore the heat may need to rise before it falls!

There are occasions when it is best not to confront a potential conflict. However, if the relationship is important to you, then it is probably best to do so: the question is when and how? If you confront the other person too soon or in the wrong way, you risk escalating the conflict, being hurt by the reaction, or provoking them to leave the situation. The first rule about confrontation is to do it when you are feeling reasonably calm and clear. If you feel this is unlikely ever to be the case, then almost certainly you need a third party to mediate the conflict. The second principle is to confront after the cooling phase if at all possible.

What is important at this stage is for each party to make clear that they recognize that the other party feels strong emotions about the issue, that they accept these emotions as valid, and that they are aware of them. Assertive methods are good coolers. Reflective comments like "I can see that you feel very angry about this" help greatly. What neither party should do at this stage is to argue back, defend, or justify their position, start an apparently logical debate on the issue, or throw new arguments and counter-arguments into the ring.

Slow the process down

Remembering the points above about win–lose, one or both parties in the conflict probably feels an intense need to end it soon, either by fighting to a conclusion or by withdrawing from the situation. Slowing the conflict down should be helped by the steps described above. In particular, if each party can hear the other's emotions without reacting or arguing back, this usually reduces the sense of pressure to get the conflict resolved one way or another. However, one or both parties may feel so emotional that they want to bring the situation to an end, and their expression of emotions may include threats to attack the other party in some way or to get out of the situation.

Feelings like the following would be quite typical at this stage:

❖ If you don't climb down and accept my demands immediately, I'll make you regret it.
❖ I've wasted enough time talking to you: I'm going to take this into my own hands now.
❖ There's no point talking to you any further. I resign.

These kind of statements typically come from a person who feels they have a weak bargaining position. They may truly have little power, for example a subordinate talking to their boss, or a supplier whose customer has many alternatives. Or they may simply feel that they have less skill in expressing themselves and handling their feelings, and be scared that they will be "talked into" a resolution that won't meet their true needs. Such statements may also be an attempt to bounce you: to push you into revealing your hand, to bring a difficult situation to a conclusion.

It is helpful if you believe that you don't have to respond to the ultimatum in the way it is put. What is more important is that you acknowledge the feelings behind the other person's statement, and if possible that you ask open questions, which give the other person the chance to keep talking about how they feel. For example: "Look, I'm really sorry you feel like that. It would help me a lot if you can explain to me why you feel that way. Can you just bear with me for a few minutes and explain this to me, please?"

Make good any loss of face

Being heard, and having your feelings reflected back by the other person, helps both parties feel that their "face" is not under threat. Once the intense emotional heat begins to reduce, aim to move to a stage where both parties can affirm the importance of their relationship with each other and can talk of things they appreciate in the other person. This sense of being valued as a person is a vital ingredient in enabling each party to feel that the conflict is about base issues and is not a personal attack on them, even though there may have been some personal put-downs earlier in the conflict.

If you can take the initiative to tell the other person how you value the relationship and what you appreciate in them, you are likely to find them starting to follow suit. It may well feel hard to take the first step, especially if you consider that the other person "started it." Try to be as specific as you can: it will help you to feel the warmth of the relationship between you. For example, recall particular times when the other person helped you out; remember early times when you were getting to know each other; appreciate specific good points from your own experience of each other.

Clarifying

This stage can begin when both parties' emotional heat has reduced to a level where mental skills can take the lead, where they can both talk about how to proceed from here and can brief each other about the issues and the needs they have. Don't be concerned if the conflict shuttles back and forth a few times between the clarifying and cooling stages!

The clarifying stage has four aims:

❖ To deal with any power and safety issues that could prevent true negotiation.
❖ To form an initial, provisional agreement on the aims, norms and process to resolve the conflict.
❖ To get all the needs and issues out "on the table" and understood by both parties.
❖ To develop an atmosphere of trust, safety, and collaboration as a basis for the third stage.

Power and safety issues

It is common for one party to feel less powerful, as described earlier. The sense of inferior power makes this party more emotionally volatile: they will feel less safe, less able to negotiate freely, partly because a feeling of low power is commonly felt as a face issue. It is up to the party with more power to take the initiative to create a sense of safety.

Ideally, part of the clarifying stage is to have each party say what they need in order to feel safe. Remember that some of the power imbalances may be perceived or emotional ones: for example one side feeling they cannot express themselves as well as the other because of a difference in formal education level. A third party facilitator is one of the best ways to deal with these types of imbalance, but simply expressing the feeling helps to diffuse it, and norms can be agreed that mitigate these problems.

Draft objectives

Seeking agreement on the outcome that both parties would like from the conflict is hopefully the start of collaboration, an opportunity for both parties to affirm the value they see in an on-going relationship and to appreciate the benefits it could give them. Mutually agreeing norms contributes to keeping the emotional heat down for the rest of the process. Here are some examples:

❖ We agree that we will only discuss this face to face and with the mediator present: we will not "negotiate" by making remarks to other people or trying to catch the other party informally in other settings.
❖ We agree to keep all of our discussions totally confidential throughout the process.
❖ If either party starts to feel emotionally threatened, they can call time out and suspend the discussions for up to 48 hours.
❖ We agree that neither party will take any action that might jeopardize the future relationship.

It is also good at this stage to seek a provisional agreement on the process for resolving the conflict. For example, an overall time period, when and how often to meet, who should be involved, who should be informed, whether to use a third party mediator, and so on.

Needs and issues

This is the central part of the clarifying stage. It should be given abundant time, several sessions if necessary. The primary aim is to know and understand all the needs and issues of both parties, not to resolve them. It is best not to insist on too much structure at this stage: the priority is to get everything on the table, including emotional needs/issues as well as mental-level ones.

As part of this stage, it can be useful to talk about how the conflict arose and why it became so emotionally heated. This enables each party to concede that they played a part in bringing the conflict about, and gets away from the adversarial or quasi-legal view that one party is guilty and "started it" and the other is an innocent victim. Ideally, by this stage both parties are able to recognize their emotional "hot buttons" and the repeating patterns that were triggered by the latest events.

The term "issues" is used here simply to mean any points of conflict between the parties. Here is one way in which the issues can be sorted into categories:

❖ *Factual issues.* Many conflicts arise or are aggravated because there is a misunderstanding or partial knowledge of the facts. For example, a bus driver does not report for duty after his car breaks down, but because of a history of absenteeism, management regards this as the last straw and takes disciplinary action without exploring all the facts.
❖ *Interest issues.* These represent the benefits or outcomes that each party wants from the negotiation.
❖ *Power issues.* These include a power imbalance between the parties, a sense that one has an unfair degree of power or that each party's rights need to be renegotiated.

❖ *Value issues.* Such issues are conflicts about whether something is right or wrong, good or bad, based on differing beliefs and values.

❖ *Face issues.* Some emotionally charged issues can affect the parties' sense of self-esteem.

These categories are in increasing order of difficulty to resolve. Putting the issues into categories like this gives a mediator, or the parties themselves, some guidelines on the order in which to tackle them, as discussed below.

Building collaboration

The experiences of having one's needs and issues heard, explored, and understood, and of working together on common tasks such as agreeing objectives, should build trust and collaboration to offset any emotional wounds from earlier in the conflict. Although resolving the issues is the work of the third stage, it is wise to aim for a few easy "early goals" in this second stage. For example, you could clear up some of the factual issues and create a sense of give and take in negotiating about the norms and the process.

Construction

The aim in this stage is for the parties to work together to construct a satisfactory solution. It can begin once all the aims of the clarifying phase have been fulfilled. It is worth having a distinct change in style or a break between sessions, since the aim in the third stage is to work creatively and collaboratively toward the final outcome of the whole process.

Anchor on the vision

If possible, harness inspirational energy explicitly in the construction process. At least, seek mutual agreement that both parties are working toward the highest good for the situation as a whole, and clarify what this means in specific terms. If negotiations look as if they are going to stall on a conflict between the interests of the two parties, invoke the question of what will serve the overall vision, the shared view of the outcome, as a way of gaining perspective.

Design future solutions

It is more fruitful to get both parties working as a team to create a new approach that meets future needs than to push along in linear, logical fashion, seeking a solution to each historical problem.

Focus on interest and power issues

Jointly designing solutions to meet future interest and power needs for both parties often enables a constructive and collaborative approach to succeed and produces a viable outcome to the overall conflict. This may mean leaving the apparently central problem—the "hot" issue that sparked the whole conflict in the first place—parked to one side. The apparent issue is often emotional, but a good process, and an outcome that meets the main interest and power needs for both parties, can diffuse the emotional issues altogether.

Mapping the situation

Focusing only on needs and problem issues can narrow the picture too much. Mapping the whole situation, not just the apparent problem, can help, for example getting each party to highlight areas of mutual agreement, disagreement, and irrelevance to the current topic. The process of mapping the whole situation can usefully bring in other parties' views and needs.

Role reversal

A powerful way to stimulate creative thinking is to get each party to role play the other's position. At the extreme, and as a "game," get each party to negotiate from the other's viewpoint. If people can suspend their attachment to their usual role and original agenda, this can unblock the process.

Try-ons

This is another way to get outside the limitations of logic and find creative solutions. A try-on means suspending or varying one apparently fixed constraint in the situation. In a wage negotiation, for example, some possible try-ons might be:

- ❖ The existing job description doesn't exist.
- ❖ There is instant, infinite development resource free of charge.
- ❖ Managers don't have to justify their actions to shareholders.

The suspension rule

As far as possible, conduct the construction phase on a mutual agreement that all preconditions are suspended and there are no fixed blocks, taboos, or assumptions to be considered.

This description offers a process to deal with a major conflict, starting from scratch. The same basic stages, in abbreviated form, are relevant in minor conflicts. For organizations it is also worth considering the creation of a conflict procedure: training some management and other staff in conflict resolution processes and setting up a means to call in their help.

Growing Your Own Toolkit

Organic farmers don't expect to anticipate every problem. They rely on the natural resilience of their soil and their systems—composting, cycles, diversity, and so on—to act as an immune system that can withstand a variety of pests and diseases without conscious, active intervention. In the same way, as you develop your own ground condition and organic ways of working, you should find that your ability to deal with problems and stress grows substantially. You may find that many issues resolve themselves "in the flow," without the need to figure out a conscious methodology. You are also likely to find that appropriate methods or tools shape themselves and emerge in the heat of the moment, as they did with Dirk Hoostra in the examples in Chapter 6. Many of the tools in this book developed this way, as real-time responses that came to me in the heat of a workshop session.

If you develop new tools for organic growth, you are welcome to share them on the bulletin board at the website for *The Natural Advantage*, www.thenaturaladvantage.com. If you would like more source books for tools, I have listed seven of my favorites below. I have started with assertiveness, because it is one of the most fundamental ingredients in managing energy and working co-creatively.

Don't say YES when you want to say NO
Herbert Fensterheim & Jean Baer, Warner, 1993.
An American self-development guide to assertiveness, looking at its application in all areas of your life, not just in your work.

Assertiveness: A Working Guide
Paddy O'Brien, Nicholas Brealey Publishing, 1990.
A good, short introduction to the subject, geared to its application in the work environment.

The Personal Management Handbook
John Mulligan, Warner, 1988.
A well-presented overview of a range of methods both for managing yourself and for relationships with others. These include tools for developing your thinking, feelings and intuition; managing stress; communication and group dynamics.

A Manager's Guide to Self-Development
Mike Pedler, John Burgoyne, & Tom Boydell, McGraw-Hill, 1994.
Designed as a self-development program, this book comes from three of the pioneers of the learning organization concept. It offers specific methods for developing many of the abilities that *The Natural Advantage* advocates, such as emotional resilience, sensitivity to events, creativity, and analytical problem solving.

Managing People in Changing Times
Robert Burns, Allen & Unwin, 1993.
Robert Burns is an Australian psychologist. This book developed from his experiences leading workshops for professional groups in business and the public sector. It has a good range of self-assessment exercises and practical tools, covering both personal and interpersonal strategies for managing change, including transactional analysis.

The Fifth Discipline Fieldbook
Peter Senge, Art Kleiner, Charlotte Roberts, Richard Ross, & Bryan Smith, Nicholas Brealey Publishing, 1994.
An excellent sourcebook both for case studies and methodologies, including such topics as systems thinking and team learning.

The Change Masters
Rosabeth Moss Kanter, International Thomson, 1992.
This book differs from the others listed here since it does not include specific tools. I have included it since it is one of my favorite books on the subject of managing change in organizations. If you start to develop organic methods within your own work, this book is especially relevant to the issues of how to foster acceptance of this kind of approach in an organization.

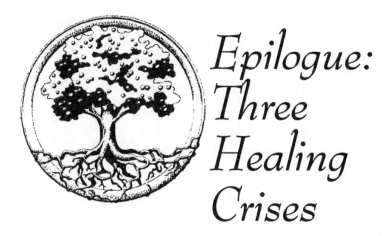

Epilogue: Three Healing Crises

Major change often arises because of a crisis. You can find many examples in this book, including Salim Hussain, Alison Martin, and Dirk Hoostra. My experience with organic growth has led me to the concept of the healing crisis: intensifying a problem in order to resolve it. The principle of the healing crisis is that the solution grows from the problem, the gold is in the muck—the issue needs to get worse before it gets better.

This is not to suggest that all organic change happens by crisis. But I do want to challenge the common notion that "naturally" means easily. The natural world is full of conflict and upheaval, as well as grace and harmony. And part of the organic way is learning to cultivate and use conflict and crisis.

One example of a healing crisis comes from the conversion period on a new organic farm: the transition from conventional methods to sustainability. A good example of a large-scale healing crisis has been the consumer revolt against genetically modified (GM) foods and the way this has reversed the views of big business and governments. I have built on such examples to offer a personal view of how three worldwide crises of sustainability will intensify and resolve. This future vision offers pointers on how you can contribute to resolving these crises on the large scale, as well as in your own work and in your organization.

The Three Crises of Sustainability

We have a global crisis of sustainability. The first field where this has become evident and acute is in the environment, but I expect this to be followed by crises of human and business sustainability. These are really three phases of addressing the one basic issue: our depleting and polluting ways of using natural resources. The same principles can resolve all three.

Accepting the need to move toward sustainability to deal with the environmental crunch will sow the seeds for the crisis of human sustainability: establishing how to work in ways that are at the same time renewing, fulfilling, and productive. As individuals make this change and demand that organizations support them, we are likely to see a much wider crisis of business sustainability. We will confront the basic questions of whether business serves the general good or just its shareholders, and whether its fruits should only be weighed in current profits. The questions of real quality, intangible benefits, and longer-term contribution will all come to the fore.

I have led many future visioning processes for businesses and individuals. One of the most powerful tools in such work is to picture the future and then envision how to get there. So open your imagination and travel forward in time to the year 2020 AD. I'd like to offer you my personal vision of how these three crises will develop and heal.

2020 vision

Under the hype about the millennium, many people in 2000 were deeply worried about the way the world was going—and with good reason. Problems such as climate, health, and the quality of our air and water have become far worse since then. Yet now in 2020, most people feel hopeful about the state of the world and its future. What has changed is that the principles of sustainability are being widely applied and the benefits are emerging. Often pollution problems took decades to build to crisis levels, and the solutions also take decades to work through. Many indicators of environmental quality are at worse levels than in 2000 and some are still rising, but we know that steps have been taken that will improve them.

People have been talking about the world environmental crisis since the 1980s, and much had been done even before the millennium. However, in the year 2000 no one could claim that our overall ways of living and working were anywhere near environmentally sustainable. Many of the crucial technologies and policy tools existed in 2000, but the will to act on them was not present. Most businesses, governments, and public opinion were still shrinking from the scale of change required.

The climate crises in developed countries tipped the balance: disasters from drought, floods, and hurricanes increased sharply from the late 1990s on. It was also clear that widespread problems were emerging for human, animal, and plant health as a result of environmental pollution. Intense public concern moved rapidly from being a minority to a majority sentiment. This change was catalyzed by several influences: the press, lobbying groups such as Friends of the Earth and the World Wide Fund for Nature, and a few major businesses that stuck their necks out and proved that a solution was possible. Eventually, public concern reached such a pitch that political leaders were obliged to act.

Healing crises: the GM model

The crisis over genetically modified foods around the turn of the century proved to be a blueprint for the wider crisis that followed. Back in 1998, a handful of retailers and food producers had been the trailblazers. In the UK the crucial move came from Iceland, the largest retailer of frozen foods. Iceland was far smaller than the leading supermarket chains, but big enough to have credibility. You could say that it represented the wild margin within the mainstream of the British food industry. It was the first substantial food retailer to state that it was possible to make its whole product range GM free, and to act on it. This was at a time when the major food manufacturers and retailers, along with the British government, were all chorusing Monsanto's line that GM foods were unavoidable: they were mixed up in everything already, so we had no option but to accept them.

Iceland's stance brought it sales increases of 20–30 percent. This was a clear enough signal to the rest of the food industry. Consumers were changing their buying behavior, not just their opinions. The following months saw an avalanche of change, as the foremost manufacturers like Unilever, plus all the leading supermarkets, dropped GM products. Once big business had altered their stance, government policy followed.

The energy revolution

When the environmental crisis reached its peak, two main changes were central to resolving it. Each depended on the governments of the leading economies worldwide introducing them together. The first of these was an eco-tax system: the burden of taxation was shifted from labor to resource use. Steep tax rises were agreed on fossil fuels and on all raw materials that were non-renewable and polluting. Manufacturers were also taxed on the disposal costs of their products. The shift to eco-taxes was phased in over 10 years, but they had a significant effect from the start. This had been forecast by Paul Hawken back in 1993, in his book *The Ecology of Commerce.*

The second crucial move was the introduction of a credible international standard for sustainability: GEN, the Global Eco Norm. This grew from pioneering work in several countries and industries, for example the German eco-standard, Der Grune Punkt, and the Forestry Stewardship Certification scheme. Like the UK Soil Association, GEN integrated the views of producers and consumers, and provided clarity amid a welter of sham eco-claims.

These two moves engendered the shift toward worldwide environmental sustainability. The form this took was essentially a revolution in energy and resource productivity. This too had been forecast in the 1990s, in books such as *Factor Four* by von Weizsacker and Lovins, and *Natural Capitalism* by Hawken and Lovins. The technologies to quadruple the wealth created per unit of natural resource were available by the millennium, but before eco-taxes business lacked the motive to commercialize them.

One significant example of this was motor vehicles. By 2010, most cars sold in the developed world were hybrid electrics: powered by electric motors, charged by an onboard generator and battery. Major car manufacturers had been developing hybrid electric designs before the millennium, and by 2005 they were stampeding on to the bandwagon and launching them into mass production. By 2010, most had gone further and introduced hypercars, combining hybrid electric drive with ultra-light materials and low-resistance tires, offering fuel consumption of 100 km per liter. Some models had already eliminated fossil fuels by using hydrogen fuel cells, and in 2020 these have become widespread.

Meanwhile, on the farm...

By the late 1990s the organic sector was growing fast in many countries, but still represented a small percentage of the market. After the millennium, this growth increased dramatically. The catalyst was the big business establishment. The early sales successes with organic foods came from the smaller national players; by 2000, the big supermarkets had noticed this and were vying with each other to expand their organic ranges. Belatedly, the multinational branded food producers joined the party. One result was the "eco-fudge" scandal: some of the larger and more cynical food giants combined to create a "Nature's Way" standard, with extravagant claims of eco-friendliness. Press exposés showed that this standard was merely a flimsy cover for intensive methods.

Consumer demand for certified organic produce kept rising. As branded products like Kellogg's Organic Cornflakes and Wall's Organic Sausages appeared, the pressure from food manufacturers to increase the supply of organic produce became desperate. This led to the super-natural movement in farming and elsewhere. Super-natural methods sought dramatic productivity rises by augmenting natural systems, not overriding them. The research teams of big food manufacturers allied with mainstream seed and farm equipment producers to work with organic farmers. As a result, plant and livestock breeds and cultivation methods evolved that gave high productivity to organic systems.

When eco-taxes steeply raised the costs of conventional farming, the profit advantage of organics became overwhelming. By 2010, a majority of farmers in developed countries had gone organic. Many others used the eco-fudge standards that still lurked at the bottom of the market.

Human sustainability: natworking

By the late 1990s, writers like Peter Senge and Arie de Geus were proposing ecology and biology as better models for the workplace than mechanics. Early in the new century, the environmental crisis took center stage; as a result, the principles and language of sustainability spread into most areas of life and work. The term "natworking" emerged to describe ways of working that aligned with human nature and were renewing and humanly sustainable.

As with previous healing crises, the issue moved from a murmur at the margins to become a mainstream debate. Several factors acted as catalysts. One was a growing number of liability lawsuits awarding hefty damages against employers for stressful and depleting work methods. Another was the pioneering companies that developed natworking approaches and proved that they also had profit benefits.

Another factor fueling the debate was the emergence of an informal international coalition called Friends of the Humans, which brought a range of interest groups together to lobby for a shift to natworking principles. These included networks of progressive companies, such as Business for Social Responsibility in the US and Tomorrow's Company in the UK. It also drew in non-profit bodies engaged with sustainable development, such as The Natural Step and Jonathon Porritt's Forum for the Future. Recognizing the impact of this issue on quality of life generally, consumer and special interest groups came in, such as Families Need Fathers. Some trade unions also joined, recognizing that adversarial campaigns for shorter hours were beside the point: the real issue was finding natural means to higher productivity.

Once more, another catalyst for change was consumers' buying behavior. To their consternation, companies found their sales affected by press exposés of their unsustainable work practices. An early example of this had been British Airways. Its harsh treatment of staff during 1997 had led to a widely publicized strike, which dented its reputation as a well-managed company. This loss of standing, coupled with poor staff morale, contributed to painful drops in market share and profits in following years.

As with the environmental crisis, the crucial change was in productivity: this time in the output value per unit of human energy and resources. Once the corporations and consultancies grasped the principles of human sustainability, there was a ferment of innovation. Natworking became the next culture fashion, and a wide range of super-natural processes and packages emerged. Fortunately, most were sound. Companies' annual reports started to feature statements on human as well as environmental sustainability, and the demand for benchmarking and objective standards grew.

Expertise in standards for organic farming and the environment was now applied to the workplace. Although it was harder to create a quality standard for human sustainability at work, this had emerged by 2010. The Green Heart symbol took its place alongside the Green Circle for environmental sustainability, both supervised by GEN. While the natworking approach was taken up by many organizations of all sizes, others spurned it. A sizable number of business leaders regarded the Green Heart standard as intrusive, a distraction from their basic economic purpose.

Toward the green dollar

Around the millennium, the stance of most big businesses on sustainability could be called clearly ambiguous. They knew that others saw it as important, so they made cosmetic moves to address it. Meanwhile, their overwhelming concern was still short-term profit. And who could blame them? This was a time when institutional investors were using their clout and firing chief executives who failed to deliver the numbers.

By 2010 the picture had changed. The big business establishment was by now evenly divided between the bottom-liners and the cultivators. Many still believed that the business of business was business: bottom-line profits. All this human sustainability talk was soft stuff—it was up to employees, not the company, to look after these issues. On the other hand, many firms were by now achieving high profits through organic principles: cultivating their people and their markets, not strip-mining them.

The wider debate about the sustainability of business started in 2010, growing out of the crisis over human sustainability at work. Views that had been on the fringe in the 1990s now reached the mainstream. Wasn't business really serving its own narrow aims and forcing consumers and governments to dance to its tune? How could the capitalist system balance the profit motive with quality of life? And if sustainable principles could apply to companies' relations with the environment and their people, surely they could apply to relations with suppliers, customers, and the wider community?

The debate was fueled because many companies, large and small, were already making good money from the sustainable approach. The bottom-liners came under fierce scrutiny. Their basic response was: We're only doing what our shareholders demand. Suddenly the focus swung round to financial institutions, and this was where the crisis erupted.

The year 2012 saw competitive turmoil in the product offerings of the pension, investment, and life assurance funds. The subject of ethical, sustainable investment took center stage. Since the 1980s there had been rapid growth in ethical funds, which screened their holdings on such criteria as no animal testing, no involvement in weapons production, and so on. By the late 1990s there was already evidence that ethical businesses were achieving better profits than many others. In 2012 this grew into the concept of the natfund: one investing only in businesses that embodied all aspects of sustainability. Most financial institutions raced to join the trend.

Before long, many bottom-line businesses were ready to change to the new agenda, but were still bewildered as to what it all meant. The Green Dollar code was developed by a coalition of business and consumer groups to answer this need. While there are still many businesses around the world fudging on standards and operating unsustainably, most of us in 2020 believe that our basic optimism is solidly grounded. We have independent proof that most firms work sustainably in most respects, and as customers we can experience this for ourselves.

Back to You

It is often said that all you can be confident of changing is your self. I strongly believe that change in organizations or society grows from change in individuals. Any steps you take toward adopting the principles of this book will help the wider move toward sustainability. Every such step adds a critical mass that will move us faster toward the resolution of the healing crises that are already here.

We have to face these wider crises, just as we all face extraordinary and increasing levels of personal change. I hope this book gives you the natural advantage to meet those pressures with fulfillment and fruitfulness.

Appendix: The Natural Step

In 1989 a Swedish cancer specialist, Karl-Henrik Robert, became concerned by the similarities between society's rapidly growing destruction of natural resources and the impact of cancer cells in the human body. He was appalled that the scientific community was having little effect on this crisis, commenting: "The scientists were like monkeys chattering amid the leaves, squabbling over details. We weren't looking for the root and trunk of the problem."

Side-stepping the debate about detailed environmental solutions, Karl-Henrik turned the process on its head. He simply kept asking: "Can we agree the basic scientific conditions for sustainability?" He began what he calls consensus debates, the first of which involved many of the leading scientists in Sweden and took 24 drafts and two years. They eventually agreed on four science principles and four system conditions for sustainability. These make up the basis of what is called The Natural Step, a set of principles and processes to identify what sustainability really means and how to move toward it. Although The Natural Step is focused on environmental sustainability, it has helped greatly with my understanding of sustainability in other fields.

The Natural Step has been widely used in business, education, and local government in Sweden, and is now being applied in the UK, US, and several other countries. Through its use many companies have achieved both business and environmental benefits. For example, McDonald's in Sweden moved itself from one of the worst to one of the best rated companies in Sweden for environmental performance. It both saved costs and added revenue, through initiatives such as more sustainable building design, heating systems, transport, and packaging. It also introduced organically produced food, as well as educational videos explaining its new approach.

Two of the main concepts in The Natural Step are the natural cycle and the four science-based principles.

The Natural Cycle

The natural cycle provides us with a basic blueprint for sustainability. It is essential for human life on Earth and provides us with our food, air, waste disposal, and much more besides.

For the first two billion years, the atmosphere on this planet was a soup of toxic gases, unsuitable for life of any kind. The crucial stage in the development of life was the evolution of green plant cells, with their capacity for photosynthesis. Plants played a central role in the slow cleaning up of the Earth's atmosphere and surface material. Over the next two billion years increasingly complex forms of animal life evolved, and eventually so did human life.

Figure 11 shows the basic elements in the natural cycle. To create their growth, green cells in plants use energy from the sun, combined with water, carbon dioxide from the air, and

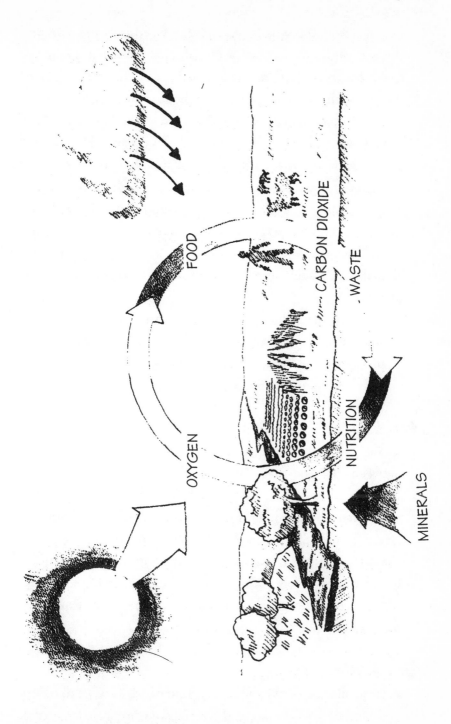

Figure 11 The natural cycle

minerals from the earth. Oxygen is produced as a by-product of this process, so plants provide two of the most essential requirements for animal and human life: oxygen and food. Plant waste returns to the soil and becomes an input to future growth.

People and animals consume oxygen as they breathe. They exhale carbon dioxide, which is recycled by plants. Human and animal waste returns to the earth and provides a further source of fertility for plant growth. Intriguingly, if we drop the concept of waste from this cycle, we can see just how balanced and productive it is: every by-product and residue serves a useful purpose. The output from plants provides the input to humans and animals, and their outputs in turn provide essential inputs to plants.

At a basic level there are three main threats to this cycle, and all are issues around waste and composting. Two are problems of the volume and type of waste being generated and the third concerns the diminishing capacity to process it.

Carbon dioxide

Global emissions of carbon dioxide more than doubled between 1965 and 1990. This is well above the recycling capacity of the planet, so we have a build-up of carbon dioxide in the atmosphere. The problems this creates include the greenhouse effect, carbon dioxide in the atmosphere preventing some of the sun's heat dispersing away from the Earth. In many cities it is also causing a reduction in the level of oxygen in the atmosphere, hence poorer air quality and an increase in respiratory diseases.

Manmade chemicals

A large number of chemicals and compounds foreign to nature are emitted into the air and water. Even in small quantities, many can have serious effects on the natural cycle. Many of them break down slowly or not at all. They disrupt nature's recycling capacity, and threaten the health of humans and all other life on the planet. For example, a chemical analysis of breast milk from healthy mothers in the US showed traces of numerous synthetic chemicals that are toxic and would never be allowed in food manufacture.

Natural recycling

Both the land area covered by forests and plants and the diversity of species are reducing sharply. This cuts the amount of human and animal waste that can be recycled, as well as lowering the resilience of the natural cycle to climate changes and new forms of waste.

Four Science Principles

The four principles in The Natural Step's basic science are summarized below. These were developed around environmental sustainability, and their application to human sustainability is explored in the following section.

Matter and energy cannot be created or destroyed

This is a principle that few scientists would dispute, yet it is quite different from the common belief that we spend or use energy, as if it disappears. In fact, energy never disappears and we don't use it up: we consume it in one form and it continues in another. For example, petrol is an exceptionally concentrated, useful form of energy. When we burn it to power a car all the energy continues, but mostly in forms that are no longer useful, such as heat emitted to the atmosphere. From this point of view, we can see that so-called waste is energy and matter in forms that we can't use. It also underlines the fact that waste will never actually disappear, it can only disperse or transform.

Matter and energy tend to disperse spontaneously

This is the Second Law of Thermodynamics, from which many of our waste and pollution problems arise. If the residual energy from using petrol in a car or fertilizer on a field remained in concentrated form, it could easily be identified and reused.

This principle highlights two essential features for a sustainable energy system:

❖ The need for an on-going energy top-up to the system, compensating for dispersal losses; we depend on the sun for this.
❖ The need for a process to harness this top-up, which is provided by green cells, discussed below.

Quality can be expressed as the concentration and structure of matter

Both quality and value are created by using energy to bring some kind of matter to a higher level of concentration, purity, and structure. For example, compare the value of polluted and purified water, crude oil and refined petroleum, earth and vegetables, raw financial data and audited accounts. This principle offers a different way of looking at waste, as matter or energy whose concentration and structure are low in quality and value.

Green cells are essentially the only net producer of concentration and structure

The green cell and its process of photosynthesis are our means of harnessing the input from the sun. Photosynthesis is essential for all human and animal life. It produces concentration and structure in both plant matter and air. This plant growth is our basic power source: it provides the energy in our food, either directly as fruit and vegetables or indirectly as animal feed; and green cells provide most of our other energy, as fossil fuel. It is also the means by which we get such life-sustaining natural services as clean air and water.

Principles of Human Sustainability

Although the four science principles describe the physical environment, they can also be applied to people. The human being is a living organism, a natural system, so it seems reasonable that our energy and sustainability will follow the same principles as the natural systems of which we are a part and on which we depend. Let's explore what the principles of The Natural Step can teach us about human sustainability.

Matter and energy cannot be created or destroyed

Does human energy come from nowhere, get used, and disappear? It seems unlikely. Whether we consider physical, emotional, mental, or inspirational energy, it is part of a cycle. Human energy has a source: we use it, change its form, create an output, and all the energy continues in some way.

Suppose my boss gets angry with me because I forgot to give a customer some information I had promised. My reaction is resentment. She didn't ask why I forgot: I was overloaded with priorities. She treated me like a machine, not a person. Still angry, I phone the customer and brusquely give them the information. The task has been done, but the atmosphere between the three of us is polluted: the negative energy has not disappeared.

This principle illuminates the concept of natural energy for the human system. It tells us that unless we use clean sources and processes, waste will accumulate.

Matter and energy tend to disperse spontaneously

The first lesson from this principle is that human energy does not sit passively in reserve, like water in a tap. Our reserves will dissipate over time. To have energy available when we need it, we have to maintain our energy flows. We need means of reconcentrating energy as well as clean sources of top-up energy. Composting can play an important role in this.

This principle also warns us that our energy residues will spread. In other words, unless it is collected and composted, human energy waste will disperse and accumulate in your body and energy system, just as environmental waste becomes pollution in earth, water, and air.

Quality can be expressed as the concentration and structure of matter

This is a powerful and different way of considering people and their work. Quality can be seen as a measure of people's well-being and productive potential, not just of their productive output. A human being is an organism whose innate quality is extraordinarily high: we represent a remarkably sophisticated concentration and structure of matter. By contrast, the quality of an intensive farm is poor: its methods progressively degrade the purity and structure of the soil and the crops. Conventional ways of working create similar quality problems.

This principle offers us a more constructive, less emotive way of viewing our waste at work. We can see it as an abundant raw material, whose quality we can improve by natural means, not as an unsightly obstacle. If you can consider yourself as a natural system and follow the principles of organic growth, you will move toward real quality in your work processes and output.

Green cells are essentially the only net producer of concentration and structure

What is the counterpart of the green cell for human energy? Drawing the analogy is tricky, since human energy is both physical and metaphysical. An emotion or an idea involves physical energy and reactions, but is more than that.

I see the whole organism—the person, team, or organization—as the equivalent of the green cell. The organism as a whole, if it operates by natural principles, can combine the four elements of human energy: physical, emotional, mental, and inspirational. Through this combination we can reconcentrate dispersed and even polluted energy, and harness the external energy inputs we need.

So what is the human equivalent of sunlight, the external energy that augments our natural system? You might ask yourself, what is the sunshine in *your* life? Where do you get a sense of natural vitality as an input? For me this comes from several sources: from my sense of purpose and service, from the love of family and friends, from job satisfaction, and from nature. The more you live out the principles of natural growth, the more clearly you will see if your energy sources are clean and sustaining or not.

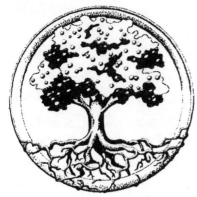 *References*

Along with direct experience and personal contacts, I have drawn on two of the standard British textbooks on organic farming. The one I would recommend to non-farmers is Francis Blake (1987) *Organic Farming and Growing*, Crowood Press, which is relatively accessible to the lay reader. Nicholas Lampkin (1990) *Organic Farming*, Farming Press, is more detailed technically and operationally, and cites a wide range of research and reference sources.

Books

de Bono, Edward (1991) *Conflicts*, Penguin.

Collins, James & Porras, Jerry (1995) *Built to Last*, Century.

Covey, Stephen (1992) *The Seven Habits of Highly Effective People*, Simon & Schuster.

Crum, Thomas (1987) *The Magic of Conflict*, Simon & Schuster.

Davis, Stan & Meyer, Christopher (1998) *Blur*, Capstone.

Edwards, Betty (1992) *Drawing on the Right Side of the Brain*, Souvenir Press (for an accessible overview and practical application of some of Roger Sperry's ideas).

Gallwey, Timothy W. (1986) *The Inner Game of Tennis*, Macmillan.

Gawain, Shakti (1979) *Creative Visualisation*, New World Library.

de Geus, Arie (1997) *The Living Company*, Nicholas Brealey Publishing.

Goleman, Daniel (1996) *Emotional Intelligence*, Bloomsbury.

Handy, Charles (1989) *The Age of Unreason*, Business Books.

Hawken, Paul (1993) *The Ecology of Commerce*, HarperCollins.

Hawken, Paul & Lovins, Amory & Hunter (1999) *Natural Capitalism*, Earthscan.

Hay, Louise (1988) *You Can Heal Your Life*, Eden Grove.

Moss Kanter, Rosabeth (1984) *The Change Masters*, Unwin Hyman.

Myers, Norman & Durrell, Gerald (1994) *The Gaia Atlas of Planet Management*, Gaia Books (for information on biodiversity).

Pascale, Richard & Athos, Anthony (1981) *The Art of Japanese Management*, Simon & Schuster.

Senge, Peter (1990) *The Fifth Discipline*, Doubleday.

Senge, Peter (1999) *The Dance of Change*, Nicholas Brealey Publishing.

Stacey, Ralph (1992) *Managing the Unknowable: Strategic Boundaries Between Order and Chaos in Organizations*, Jossey-Bass.

von Weizsacker, Ernst & Lovins, Amory & Hunter (1997) *Factor Four*, Earthscan.

Other sources

data

For information about open workshops on The Natural Advantage with Alan Heeks and colleagues and about tailored programs for organizations, contact Working Vision, ~~PO Box 13, Stockbridge SO20 6WR, UK. Tel: +44 (0)1794 388707~~, email: ~~mail~~@workingvision.com, website: www.workingvision.com. *The WorkEasy Workbook* by Alan Heeks is available by mail order from Working Vision.

The Wessex Foundation/Magdalen Farm Centre: information on the project, programs, and facilities from Magdalen Farm Centre, Winsham, Chard, Somerset TA20 4PA, UK. Tel: +44 (0)1460 30144, email: wessex@magdalencentre.freeserve.co.uk, website: www.magdalencentre.freeserve.co.uk.

Alibi and several of the other cases described in this book involved extensive use of coaching. If you want to get contact details for a professional coach in your area, Coach-U is an international organization of professional coaches, website: www.CoachU.com.

For information on The Natural Step contact Det Naturliga Steget, Wallingatan 22, SE-111 24 Stockholm, Sweden. Tel: +46 8 789 29 00, fax: +46 8 789 29 39, website: www.detnaturligasteget.se. Or in the UK contact The Natural Step, 9 Imperial Square, Cheltenham GL50 1QB. Tel: +44 (0)1242 262744.

If you want an intensive process professionally facilitated to help you compost major problems, I recommend the Hoffman Institute, which operates in the UK, USA, and elsewhere. Details via their website: www.quadrinity.com. UK tel: +44 (0)800 0687114.

Business for Social Responsibility, 609 Mission St, 2nd Floor, San Francisco CA 94105-3106, USA. Tel: +1 415 537 0888, fax: +1 415 537 0889, email: memberservices@bsr.org, website: www.bsr.org.

Business in the Community, 44 Baker St, London W1M 1DH, UK. Tel: +44 (0)20 7224 1600.

Centre for Tomorrow's Company, 19 Buckingham St, London WC2N 6EF, UK. Tel: +44 (0)20 7930 5150, website: www.tomorrowscompany.com.

Forum for the Future, 227A City Rd, London EC1V 1JT, UK. Tel: +44 (0)20 7477 7730, website: www.forumforthefuture.org.uk.

Soil Association, Bristol House, 40–56 Victoria Street, Bristol BS1 6DY, UK. Tel: +44 (0)1179 290661, email: info@soilassociation.org, website www.soilassociation.org.

Index